Getting Together and Staying Together:

The Stanford University Course on Intimate Relationships

Getting Together and Staying Together:

The Stanford University Course on Intimate Relationships

By

Thomas Plante, PhD
and
Kieran Sullivan, PhD

1stBooks-rev. 02/23/01

About the Book

<u>Rationale and Overall Purpose</u>

A tremendous amount of media attention has been directed towards intimate relationships. Magazine articles, books, television specials have all focused on what makes intimate relationships work or not work. There are hundreds of books on this topic. However few books have well integrated the academic and clinical aspects of relationships specifically for those trying to find a life partner and to maintain a lifelong commitment.

For the past 13 years, we have been teaching courses on intimate relationships at a variety of universities, including Stanford University, the University of California, Los Angeles, the University of Kansas, Santa Clara University, and Loyola Marymount University. The purpose of the book is to essentially turn this popular course into an easy to read, understand, and use book for the general public and as a supplement to undergraduate and graduate courses in intimate relationships and counseling.

What makes this book different is that it offers a concise, practical, and straightforward approach to intimate relationships that is based on both scientific research and clinical practice. Written by two full-time academics who maintain part-time clinical practices, the book provides the balance between research and practice that is needed for this topic.

Table of Contents

Preface

Involvement in intimate relationships is one of the most fundamental and universal facets of life. Intimate relationships fulfill many basic human needs (e.g., for love, passion, companionship, etc.) and are the process through which we pass on our genes, our knowledge, and our values to the next generation. Intimate relationships are of great interest to us because they help to define who we are and how we will live our lives. Good relationships can enhance every aspect of our lives and bad relationships can be equally destructive. Because of this, people have examined and given advice about intimate relationships for thousands of years. This is reflected in literature, art, theater, music, and, more recently, through psychological studies about what makes relationships work (and not work).

The scientific study of intimate relationships is relatively new, psychology itself has only been around for about 100 years. Likewise, the clinical practice of couples therapy is a relatively young practice, developing alongside the science of psychology, becoming widespread only about 40 years ago. In this time, however, hundreds, perhaps thousands, of studies have been done on intimate relationships and many different forms of treating distressed couples have been developed and tested. The study of intimate relationships is an exciting and dynamic field, constantly providing new information and new, more effective treatments to help prevent and treat relationship problems.

Perhaps the biggest problem in the field is that there are few avenues to bring information learned in the laboratory and in clinical practice to people other than fellow professionals: to students interested in intimate relationships, to practitioners, and to the general public. Relationship researchers typically publish in scientific journals that are not easily accessible or understandable to non-scientists. Though there are a few exceptions, for the most part our professional knowledge and experience have remained locked up in the "ivory tower." This seems particularly tragic, given the high rate of divorce and the general need for the best information about how to relate successfully to others. Unfortunately, most people tend to get information from "popular" psychology books, which are often based on one person's personal experience of intimate relationships, or, at best, one person's clinical experience with couples in therapy. These books are often not helpful, or at worst, can be destructive by passing out misinformation that hurts rather than helps relationships.

This book is designed to present accurate information about close relationships based on both scientific knowledge and clinical practice. It begins by presenting information about interpersonal attraction and finding a mate, and evolves into an examination of what makes a relationship work once you have found one. Most chapters present empirical information illustrated by case examples about such topics as why relationships are so important, attraction, love, sex and passion, commitment, and marriage. Also included are chapters that present practical suggestions on how to find a mate, how to make your relationship work, and how to find help for your relationship when you need it.

This book is different from other books on intimate relationships in several ways. First, as previously mentioned, the book is based on an integration of psychological research on and clinical experience with intimate relationships. This approach was adopted to help ensure that scientific information is presented in a way that is both accurate and easy to understand. Second, the information presented is drawn from several fields, including sociology, evolutionary psychology and clinical psychology. Many books on intimate relationships are restricted to only one of these approaches. By drawing from all of these fields, we can provide a more complete picture of the entire developmental process of relationships, from finding partners, to dating, to marriage, and ultimately to dealing with marital difficulties. Third, this book takes a biopsychosocial approach. This is a more holistic approach that explains phenomena such as gender differences as an interaction of biological and genetic factors, psychological factors, and socio-cultural factors.

It is our hope that this book can be useful for the millions of Americans who deal with the challenges and joys of intimate relationships everyday.

Chapter 1
Introduction

Why bother writing another book on intimate relationships when there seem to be billions of them on the bookshelves? It is a good question. Any Psychology or Self Help section of any large bookstore seems to have hundreds of books published by psychotherapists and others about intimate relationships. While browsing in bookstores, we often find ourselves reviewing many of these books and usually have several reactions. One is amusement. Often these books have a large picture of the author (usually looking very glamorous) and a description of their intimate relationship qualifications (e.g., licensed psychotherapist, learned a great deal from their own divorce, appeared on Donahue and Oprah). It seems amazing that being on the day time talk show circuit somehow implies that you must really know your stuff. Furthermore, some of these writers seem to spend more time in self promotion than anything else. Some come into the field of psychology from other areas and often have little psychological research background, going almost immediately into practice and/or writing self help books.

Another reaction is, "does this stuff really help anyone"? Given how popular these books are, we'd like to hope so. After all, about 50% of all first marriages end in divorce (and second and third marriages have even higher divorce rates!) and it appears that there are a lot of unhappy relationships out there. Furthermore, it is hard to believe that the other 50% of first marriages that never divorce are all blissfully happy. Therefore, there is a huge number of people looking to the "experts" for help in improving and enhancing their intimate relationships.

Our concern about the numerous books on intimate relationships is that too many are based on "pop psychology." Too often they are based on some particular therapist's or self proclaimed expert's view of life and love. Rarely are they based on scientific data or solid clinical experience. Some books are written by scholars and do a good job at discussing the research data on intimate relationships. However, we find that many of

1

these books are pretty dry and boring, with little practical help for the average reader. Some of these books are pretty esoteric. For example, while scholarly and excellently written, some examine the relationships of animals or ancient humans in great detail and then make inferences about current human relationships. We've enjoyed reading many of these books. We have found them intellectually challenging and compelling but not very helpful from a practical standpoint.

So why write another intimate relationships book? We believe that the time has come for a book that is both "user-friendly" and based on scholarly research. It is our desire to write a book that makes the often complex psychological research on intimate relationships available for the people who need to know the results the most: people struggling to have successful intimate relationships. We have spent a lot of time researching intimate relationships professionally, treating couples with difficulties in their intimate relationships, and translating the scientific knowledge and our experience into classes on intimate relationships. Together, we have taught courses on Intimate Relationships at five different universities: Stanford University, Santa Clara University, University of California, Los Angeles, University of Kansas, and Loyola Marymount University. We find these courses to be both personally rewarding and extremely popular with students. They find that the academic study of intimate relationships is both intriguing in itself and extremely practical for their own lives. We feel that writing a book that conveys the information discussed in these popular classes could be useful for many others as well. We hope that it is.

What makes this book different from the millions on the market? We think that offering a concise, practical, and straightforward book on intimate relationships that is based on both clinical practice and scientific research is somewhat unique. Also, a book by full time academics who maintain part-time clinical practices provides the balance between research and practice that is really needed for this topic.

Rarely does one say on one's deathbed, "I wish I spent more time at the office." When it comes right down to it, our intimate

2

relationships are what much of life seems to be all about. We hope that this book sheds some light on this critical topic.

Chapter 2
Why are Intimate Relationships So Important?

Intimate relationships are remarkably important, perhaps more than we acknowledge or know. Why is this the case? In a country that so highly values independence and doing "your own thing," why are intimate relationships so profoundly critical to not only our happiness but our very survival?

Definition

First, let's define what we mean by "intimate relationships". Sandra Brehm, in her book <u>Intimate Relationships</u>, defines intimate relationships as having three important components:

     (1) emotional attachment
     (2) interdependence
     (3) fulfillment of needs

Though relationships differ in terms of their intensity, level of commitment, emotion, sexuality, and gender, all intimate relationships involve all three components at least to some degree.

Emotional Attachment

Intimate relationships involve emotional attachment. Feelings are involved. Expecting that love can be found if someone meets all of our rational criteria (e.g., good job, shared interests, shared religious faith, physically appealing) in a checklist fashion is not enough to develop the feelings of emotional attachment. Emotions certainly do not always follow the rigors of logic. For example, one of us once saw a woman, we'll call her "Emma," in therapy. During her treatment, she struggled with deciding whether or not to continue her relationship with her boyfriend, "Jason". They had been dating for several years and she found him lacking many of the things she had hoped for in a partner. He wasn't very intellectually stimulating or particularly thoughtful of her needs. He often forgot important dates, such as their anniversary, and sometimes left for days following a fight. When the therapist asked why she stayed with him, she would invariably reply "because I love him." What she seemed to mean when she said this was that she was emotionally attached to him and sexually drawn to him. He "made her heart beat faster" when he walked in the room. The situation was especially confusing because there was another man who was interested in Emma, "David." David was a coworker and seemed to be everything Jason was not: stable, thoughtful, and very interesting. But Emma had no feelings for David, even though she knew intellectually that he might be a better match for her than Jason. She continued to stay in her relationship with Jason, because he was the one she loved - the one she had an emotional attachment to.

Interdependence

Interdependence of partners means that when one acts, it has an effect on the other and the other, in turn, reacts. It is what psychologists and other mental health professionals call a "systems view." The partners are not two independent units but are interdependent on each other, constantly acting and reacting to each other as in an elaborate dance. In fact, we tend to have much stronger reactions to our intimate partners than with acquaintances, friends, and even other family members. This makes sense, because the actions, thoughts and beliefs of our intimate partners can have a much more profound effect on us than those of any other person. The longer we are in a relationship, the more this is true. For example, whether our friend believes it is wrong to live with a person before marriage, or to send her children to a particular school, or to eat meat may be interesting to us, but will not really affect our lives. But if our dating partner or spouse believes those things, this can have a profound effect on our lives, especially if we don't believe them!

With interdependency comes the need to trust the other and to feel somewhat comfortable with vulnerability. Trust, not easy for many who have had abusive or highly conflictual relationships in the past, is essential for partners. You must be able to trust that your partner will be faithful, will keep your interests and well being in mind, and will not try to hurt you. Being vulnerable means that the closer you get to your partner, the more vulnerable you become to rejection and loss. If the relationship ends, the pain is likely to be felt most intently if there was a high degree of trust, vulnerability, and intimacy.

FULFILLMENT OF NEEDS
Relationships fulfill many needs, including intimacy. Relationships also help us to integrate into the social environment (we go out with our partner, bring them with us to parties, etc.). They also provide us with nurturance, and a person whom we can nurture. Having a relationship partner can also be of great assistance with the practical aspects of life (e.g., food shopping, clothes washing), and help to reassure us of own self worth. Clearly, intimate relationships fulfill many needs, not just our need for sex and companionship.

THE BIOPSYCHOSOCIAL MODEL
Ever since Rene Descartes's famous philosophy of dualism (the split between the mind and the body) in the 17th century, we have tended to think about our bodies and our psyches as two separate entities. There are many examples today that illustrate our tendency to think things are caused by biology (our bodies) or psychology (our minds and our behaviors). We wonder whether homosexuality is due to environmental influence or some gene or brain tissue. We want to know if obesity is caused by a gene or by eating too much. If we have unexplained pain we want to know if it's "all in our head" or if it is due to some biological lesion (e.g., brain tumor). This either/or nature vs nurture debate has gone on for centuries. While there has been a movement during the past several decades for a more holistic approach to medicine and other fields, for the most part, two separate camps still exist: those who view biology and genetics are at the root of our being and those who believe that who we are is fundamentally a result of our experiences.

This debate has found its way into discussions about intimate relationships. While pretty much everyone agrees that men and women are different in their approaches to relationships, what is debated is whether these differences are due to biological differences between the sexes or due to the different cultural and environmental influences on little girls versus little boys. One biological theory that has received a lot of attention lately uses an evolutionary perspective. Evolutionary psychologists such as David Buss from the University of Michigan and anthropologists such as Helen Fisher from the American Museum of Natural History in New York report that much of our problems and experiences with intimate relationships can be traced to evolutionary influences. For example, Helen Fisher explains the fact that divorces occur as often as they do and when they do (after about four years of marriage) because in our evolutionary past, about four years were needed to conceive and raise a child to a minimal level of independence, at which point the clan could then continue helping with child rearing. Fisher and others explain infidelity as evolutionarily helpful in that spreading our genes around by mating with a number of partners will likely keep our genes from dying out. Maximizing reproductive success and continuing the species is more likely if people mate often and with a variety of partners. While these researchers provide compelling explanations for human intimate relationships from studying the behavior of animals and our own evolutionary past, one problem with this approach is that it implies that human behavior is driven by biological forces that cannot be helped. Therefore, we can't be held responsible for causing the pain that infidelity brings to our spouses and our children. We are simply biologically hardwired to have sex with others outside of the marriage relationship in order to maximize reproductive success! Few jilted husbands or wives today would be likely to find this highly convenient argument compelling.

On the other hand, trying to explain the differences between men and women by saying they are only a result of our different upbringings is not compelling either. It ignores too much evidence of biological differences. It's the either/or thinking that has led to many problems with the nature-nurture debate. This either/or thinking is also at the heart of numerous debates about intimate relationships focusing around questions concerning why women behave as they do while men behave as they do. For example, one might ask: "Why do so many men have trouble making a commitment?" or "Why do men want to reach orgasm so much quicker than their female partners?" The biopsychosocial model was developed to provide a more sophisticated and useful way of viewing these important issues and questions.

George Engel, a well known and respected researcher and psychiatrist, offered the biopsychosocial model in a paper he published in the prestigious journal Science in 1977. He suggested that physical symptoms of illness could be better understood and treated if the traditional medical view that the problem must be *either* physical *or* psychological was not used. Instead, the most helpful way to diagnosis and treat an illness is to keep in mind the biological, psychological, and social aspects of the illness and its treatment, and how all these forces interact to keep people sick or help them get well. This model has been vigorously endorsed by many professional groups and organizations such as the Society of Behavioral Medicine, an interdisciplinary group of physicians, psychologists, nurses, and other health care professionals. However, still today, while many professionals provide lip service to the biopsychosocial model, many still resort to the Descartes and Newton dualism of the 17th century.

How does the biopsychosocial model help us to better understand intimate relationships? In looking at the numerous questions and issues involved in satisfying intimate relationships, we must examine and consider the biological, psychological, and social influences. The integration of these three influences are more likely to shed light on our relationship questions and concerns than one or two of these perspectives. While this might seem obvious, we rarely do it. For example, in examining the common view that men have more trouble with commitment than women, it is too simplistic to state that this might be solely due to either genetic or child rearing influences. Consider President Clinton. His is a high profile case of a man's infidelity, even under circumstances that put him at extreme risk (of losing political power, his place in history as a president, etc.). People have offered a number of explanations for his conduct, including Monica Lewinsky's seductive behavior, marital problems, and the temptations that go along with being in

9

a powerful position. Though we can never really know what went on, it seems silly to assume that his behavior was due to his "just being a man" (certainly there are many men who do not commit adultery) or because Monica was so compelling (there are also many men who do not pursue attractive or seductive women because they are married) or because he was seduced by power (there are certainly many powerful men who remain faithful to their wives) or because he and Hilary didn't have a satisfactory sexual relationship (many men who are unhappy with their marital relationships do not try to solve the problem through adultery). It seems far more likely that his behavior was multiply determined, that is, there were many factors that interacted with each other and led to his sexual promiscuity. Considering the biological, psychological, and social influences are more likely to help us understand relationship phenomenon with more precision. The biopsychosocial model will be referred to and utilized throughout this book.

THE IMPORTANCE OF RELATIONSHIPS

Sigmund Freud used to say that what life was all about was "love and work". But in the United States, we seem to focus more on work than love. It is well known that people seem to be working more in the United States than ever before and taking fewer and fewer vacations. Compared to England, Germany, Italy, France, and many other countries, we spend much less time outside of the work environment. Plus many of our modern conveniences such as fax machines, cellular phones, computers, overnight delivery all seem to raise work expectations for efficiency and productivity rather than making our lives more leisurely. Thus increased focus on work might appear to detract from the time and energy we spend on personal relationships, but this turns out not to be the case. In fact, it is a mistake to separate the two, because even in the work place, we focus on relationships quite a bit. If you listen to people discuss their work, often discussions lead to relationships, with co-workers, the boss, and subordinates. How well we do at work is dependent, at least in part, on how well we relate to other human beings. Relationships are fundamental to many aspects of our lives, including work.

Further, when we are able to step back and look at the big picture, we can see that relationships are at least as important as work, if not more so. When you think about it, few people probably look back on their lives on their deathbeds and wish they had spent more time at the office.

Yet paradoxically, while relationships are so critical, we typically "wing it" when it comes to developing and nurturing relationships. We often can be very thoughtful and planful about our educational or career goals or about other aspects of our lives. But we are rarely very thoughtful or planful about our relationships. For example, thinking that you might find a partner or "the one and only" randomly in a bar, a gym, at a shopping mall, etc. is rather odd. Most would consider it silly to find a job merely by going randomly from business to business looking for work. Many people take better care of their car, plants, or pets than they do nurturing their intimate relationships. Somehow we think, not very rationally, that it will all just work out wonderfully without any work or effort.

Another important point is that we often know how to secure satisfying relationships but we just can't seem to do it. Similarly, we typically all know how to maintain a normal weight (i.e., exercise regularly and minimize high fat and caloric foods) as well as a variety of other health behaviors (drinking alcoholic beverages in moderation, brushing and flossing teeth regularly, drinking plenty of water, etc.) yet we have a hard time doing it. In a Health Psychology course at Santa Clara University, undergraduates are instructed to develop a self change program to improve one health behavior during the quarter. Examples include eating more fruits or vegetables, eating less fatty foods, flossing teeth, wearing seat belts regularly, increasing exercise, etc. They conduct this project using all of the latest technology and ideas about behavior change. Very few are successful in significantly changing their behavior by the end of the term and beyond. While they are intelligent and motivated students, they report that stress, illness, work, etc, interfere with their good intentions. The same is true for relationship development. We may start out intending to work conscientiously on finding a mate and working hard to make sure our intimate relationships go well once we find a partner. But all these good intentions seem to disappear when reality hits.

WHAT MAKES SUCCESSFUL RELATIONSHIPS SO DIFFICULT?

Research from numerous disciplines using a wide variety of research methodologies has underscored time and time again the importance of early relationships. The famous studies conducted by Harry Harlow from the University of Wisconsin demonstrated that comfort derived from contact with their care takers is more important even than food! In these studies, young monkeys are fed by a fake wire-mesh "mother" but also have available a fake "mother" monkey covered with terry cloth. Though the terry cloth mothers do not feed the young monkeys, they spend the majority of their time clinging to the soft mothers and minimal time in contact with the food-providing wire-mesh monkeys. Famous studies in the 1940's by Spitz demonstrated a similar phenomena in humans. Spitz followed numerous orphaned children, and found that the infants who were deprived of loving human contact often died or became physically or emotionally disabled (even when all of their basic needs for food, water, cleanliness, etc, were adequately taken care of!). More recent research by well known authors such as John Bolby and Daniel Stern have also indicated how critical early attachment with others is for later physical and emotional development. Research with mice and other animals has demonstrated that touch is absolutely necessary for survival. Mice raised without touch from their mother (even though all physical needs such as food and water were met) were more likely to die than mice who were allowed touch from their mother.

Erik Erikson, a well known psychoanalyst, developed a theory of human development that includes eight stages. In each stage, we are confronted with a dilemma. If we deal with the dilemma well, we develop an important virtue that we carry with us throughout life. For example, when we are about one or two years old, we begin to try to do things for ourselves. We begin to grasp objects that we want and gradually learn to eat, play and even go to the bathroom ourselves. During this period, we will experience successes and failures. Depending on how our caretakers respond, we will either feel independent and capable or doubtful about our abilities. If we successfully achieve independence, or *autonomy* during this period, we will attain the virtue of will - the ability to have enough confidence and independence to carry out our desires. If we do not successfully achieve autonomy, we may be riddled with doubt when we try to accomplish our will throughout our lives. All of Erikson's stages and their corresponding virtues, are listed below

Erik Erikson's Eight Stages of Psychosocial Development

Stage	Age	Virtue
1. Trust vs Mistrust	0-1	Hope
2. Autonomy vs Doubt	1-2	Will
3. Initiative vs Guilt	3-5	Purpose
4. Industry vs Inferiority	6-12	Competence
5. Identity vs Role Confusion	13-19	Fidelity
6. Intimacy vs Isolation	20-35	Love
7. Generativity vs Stagnation	35-50	Care
8. Ego Integrity vs Despair	50-	Wisdom

While many of these stages have implications for our ability to have successful relationships as adults, three are particularly important in understanding why it is that some people are more successful than others. The first of these is the stage of trust vs mistrust. This is the stage we all go through as infants. As infants, we experience important needs, such as the need for food, for comfort, for cleanliness. When we are feeling one of these needs, our caretakers may respond immediately or they may not. The extent to which our needs are met on a regular basis teaches us about the nature of the world and other people, as trustworthy or not. If our needs are not met on a fairly regular basis, we may have difficulty trusting others as adults. It is important to keep in mind that the difficulties during this stage (and all of the stages) do not necessarily doom us in later life.

Our experiences in each stage do, however, provide a framework and a filter through which we perceive our future experiences in life.

Another stage that may have important implications for our ability to relate to others is the fifth stage, which occurs in adolescence. During this time we form our personal identities, our basic understanding of who we are as a person. A strong sense of personal identity is crucial for later relationship development. Without a strong sense of who we are, it is difficult to know who we should be with, who would be a good choice for the type of person we are. Further, once we are in a relationship, confusion about who we are will likely make the relationship confusing as well, for ourselves and for our partners.

Once we emerge from adolescence and have a fairly firm sense of our own identities, we then enter the stage of development where intimate relationships form: Intimacy vs Isolation. During this stage, according to Erikson and others, we develop intimate personal relationships. Occurring in young adulthood, this is when we seek a life partner and when the large majority of people marry. How well we accomplish this is based, in large part, on the outcome of the stages we went through before. These previous stages of development set the foundation for adult intimate relationships to develop.

In conclusion, we can see that our experiences growing up and how we handle these experiences can affect our ability to have satisfying, close relationships as adults. But just understanding the stages of development does not explain the process that occurs when we have trouble developing and nurturing satisfying intimate relationships. To better understand this, researchers have studied people who have trouble with relationships and identified the factors that are typically associated with our inability to negotiate a satisfying intimate relationship.

The following is a list of the typical factors that contribute to our inability to maintain satisfying intimate relationships:

Common Problems with Intimate Relationships

---

1. Fears of abandonment and betrayal
2. Fear of loss of autonomy and self, fear of closeness, fear of engulfment
3. Fear of damage
4. Strains of sexuality that neutralize tenderness (need to dominate, inflict harm)
5. Self defeating, masochistic inspired (need to be punished)
6. Inability to idealize or overidealize
7. Inability to trust
8. Less structure imposed by church and community, increased expectations of relationships, stress of life

---

Many of us experience at least some of the fears or limitations listed above. They are rooted in our earlier relationships and development. Experiencing these things does not automatically mean that you will have significant difficulties finding a mate or maintaining a good relationship. But if you experience these feelings or thoughts intensely enough, it can interfere with your ability to have a successful relationship. Most of the items listed above involve fears of being hurt, inability to trust, emotional difficulties, or unrealistic expectations. The vast majority of relationship problems can be traced to one or more of these difficulties. Knowing your weaknesses in these areas (and those of your partner) are an important step towards attempting to develop a satisfying relationship.

Fear of being hurt. It is true that the more we love someone, the more we are vulnerable to being hurt. This fundamental truth about love was portrayed quite poignantly in the movie "Shadowlands," which was based on the life of C.S. Lewis, a famous author and professor at Oxford University. Mr. Lewis, though very accomplished and admired, lives a safe and protected life, teaching students who dare not challenge him and living a comfortable bachelor existence with his brother. Late in life, he falls in love with Joy, an outspoken New York divorcee, because she challenges him. She makes him realize that he has never experienced the most important aspects of life (love, intimacy, attachment) though he has written about them eloquently in his books. However, just as he begins to learn to truly love, he must face the loss of Joy through cancer. He struggles with whether it really was better "to have loved and lost than never to have loved at all." With Joy's help, he comes to accept that he is fundamentally a better person, and more human, for having had Joy in his life.

Many people struggle with this question, especially if they have experienced hurt in their past by people they have loved. Opening yourself up to love is particularly difficult if you experienced abandonment as a child, either through death or physical or emotional separation from your caretakers. A critical first step to being able to open yourself up to love again may be to take the time to truly mourn the loss or losses you have experienced before. Coming to terms with previous abandonments or betrayals will help loosen their power over you and help to prepare you for the risk of loving again.

Fear of loss of autonomy and self, fear of closeness, fear of engulfment. People with these fears have often had the opposite experience of abandonment, the experience of being overly "loved" and smothered by people in their past. Previous partners or even caretakers may have been overly dependent and demanding of their time and energy, leaving them drained and overwhelmed. We knew of one young man, "Greg" who had been avoiding relationships and even dating for years for these very reasons. One of his first serious girlfriends, "Cyndi," was sweet and charming, with a great sense of humor. Unfortunately, she struggled with depression, which worsened over the course of their 2½ years together. Greg was very supportive and loving, and tried to do everything he could to help her, including helping her with money and car rides to psychotherapy. Cyndi had a particularly strong depression and gradually became more and more dependent on Greg, both financially and emotionally. Greg begin charging her antidepressant medication on his credit cards (which he could not afford) and spending hours on the phone with Cyndi trying to comfort her. Finally, he became so completely overwhelmed that he ended the relationship. Because of Cyndi's illness, he had to struggle with a lot of guilt for a long time before he was finally able to end it. Because of this experience, Greg proceeded to avoid any kind of contact with women for a long time. He was afraid that if he started to care for someone, he would end up getting overly involved and overwhelmed again.

Fear of damage. In the above example, Greg experienced some damage as a result of his relationship with Cyndi. His self-esteem was eroded because he felt guilty about leaving her. He lost confidence in his ability to meet and maintain a relationship with someone healthy. He even incurred quite a bit of financial damage in the process. This fear of damage is another reason why people avoid becoming close to another.

Strains of sexuality that neutralize tenderness. Another factor that can limit people's ability to maintain an intimate relationship is strains of sexuality that do not promote intimacy and commitment. These may include the need to dominate or inflict harm on sexual partners in order to achieve sexual gratification. Though most people have sexual fantasies and even urges that are outside of the "mainstream," if the need to act in a way that is damaging to tenderness and trust is overwhelming, it can seriously limit the development of intimate relationships. Lovers need to keep in mind that, while sexual gratification is important, the trust and tenderness in the relationship must be the first priority. As relationships develop, sharing fantasies and desires within the context of a trusting relationship can enhance both sexuality and the relationship.

Self defeating, masochistic inspired (need to be punished). Likewise, people who approach relationships and/or sexuality in a masochistic or self-defeating way are also going to have trouble developing true intimacy. Approaching a relationship, sexually or otherwise, as if you are less than and deserve maltreatment will preclude you from being able to develop an adult relationship of two equals. Self-respect is a must in relationships, without it, others (especially your partner) will not have respect for you, making any kind of true intimacy impossible.

Inability to idealize or overidealize. As discussed previously, in order to be able to overcome fear and commit yourself to a long-term relationship, you must have the capacity to idealize your partner. It is not unlike having a baby. Most people who get pregnant (intentionally, anyway) do so with an idealized, even overidealized, view of what their life will be like when the baby comes. They picture a beautiful baby, sleeping peacefully, smiling up at them. They imagine feeling closer than ever before to their spouse. In reality, however, we know that having a baby can be very difficult. Babies cry, wake up in the night, and change our lives completely. They are also very expensive. Researchers also know that when a couple has a baby, relationship satisfaction actually goes way down. If couples fully realized all this information, they might not be so eager to get pregnant! But that would be a problem for the human species. So we are primed to see babies as very cute and desirable, to overidealize, so that we will continue to reproduce. So it is with relationships as well. We enter relationships with an idealized vision of our partner. If you are unable to idealize partners or potential partners, you may not ever choose to begin or maintain an intimate relationship.

Inability to trust. The inability to trust you partner can be poisonous to a relationship. Inability to trust is often accompanied by jealousy. Though jealousy is something we all experience and is quite normal, if it occurs too often, or with too much intensity, it can erode any relationship. An amusing example appears on a recent T.V. advertisement. A suspicious husband returns home in the middle of the day to surprise his wife. He finds a strange car parked outside and sees his wife through the window, talking to a man he does not know. Being a construction worker, he is driving a cement truck. He proceeds to fill the strange car (a convertible) with cement. Just as the car is completely filled, his wife comes out of the house and says, "Honey, this is the car salesman. He brought over your birthday present. Surprise!" He has ruined his own brand new convertible. Jealous and lack of trust can be just as destructive to a relationship. When you send the message that you do not trust your partner, you are sending the message that your partner is not trustworthy. This is deeply insulting and hurtful to a partner who truly loves you and is faithful to you.

Less structure imposed by church and community, increased expectations of relationships, stress of life. This last factor is less personal and has more to do with changes in the communities in which we live. In the last few decades, social changes have occurred that make the maintenance of intimate relationships harder than ever before. Divorces are less stigmatized and much easier to get. There are fewer and fewer support structures to help couples stay together. At the same time, we continue to have very high expectations of relationships. We believe that our relationships should bring us constant happiness, sexual gratification, and friendship. Finally our lives are becoming more and more stressful, for both individuals and families. We work long hours and take short vacations. Many more women are working and adequate childcare can be difficult to find and expensive. Thus we need more support than ever, but the support seems much harder to find. All of these social changes take their toll on intimate relationships.

CONCLUSION

Relationships are a fundamental part of our lives, yet they are often difficult to find and difficult to keep. These difficulties arise from our own hurts and shortcomings as well as from the changing society in which we live. To find and keep a healthy relationship, it is important to be aware of our fears and past hurts. We need to take inventory of our lives and address our fears and early losses in order to prepare ourselves to love. We also need to realize that our society is not always as supportive of relationships as it has been in the past. Therefore we need to find supportive people and communities to help us, sometimes in finding a partner and sometimes in keeping our relationships together. Though it takes a lot of work, relationships are definitely worth it. Emotional attachment and interdependency with another is one of the most basic, and one of the most rewarding, aspects to being alive.

Chapter 3
Attraction

LOVE MAPS

What is it about someone that makes you take a second look, that gives you that longing feeling in the pit of your stomach, that makes your socks roll up and down with excitement? You look across a crowded room spotting someone who you instantly feel love and longing for; How does that work? Is there such a thing as love at first sight? How can we feel love and longing for someone we know nothing about?

One theory that explains this type of immediate attraction is that we all carry around with us an "attraction template" or a "love map". This is a template of basic qualities that we have come to think is a good match for us. People's templates vary, for example, a young man who is very involved in sports might find active women attractive or a shy man might look for an outgoing woman. As we see various people throughout our day, a very quick cognitive process occurs where we compare the person we have seen with our individual template. In doing so, we decide, almost instantaneously, whether that particular person is attractive or unattractive to us. When we encounter someone that seems to match our attraction template, we immediately take notice. This is typically true whether we are involved in an intimate relationship or not, whether we are happy in our relationship or not, and whether we are looking to meet a potential partner or not.

As we learn more and more about a potential mate, we continue to compare them with our attraction template. Imagine you see someone at a social or work event or perhaps just walking on the street. You notice that they are very attractive to you. Perhaps you even notice some sexual arousal and longing to be with that person. Suppose more information becomes available to you about this person. You hear them speak, you see them light a cigarette, you find out a little more detail. With each detail you reassess their attractiveness to determine whether they continue being in the center of your attraction template or if they are no longer appealing to you.

Curiously, we project our wishes, fantasies, and desires onto this stranger almost immediately after noticing them. For example, we may have some ideas about their personality, what they do for a living, their likes and dislikes all from a glance. As small bits of information from reality unfold, our hypotheses about the person are confirmed or denied. For example, one woman described a brief courtship she had in college with a fellow student, Mike. The woman was religious, liberal, bright, and a very good student. She had noticed Mike in the cafeteria and felt immediately drawn to him. As she learned from mutual friends that he was also quite religious, she felt her attraction to him grow. She began to imagine him as also very bright, liberal and as a good student. When he asked her out, she consented enthusiastically. Throughout dinner, she talked to him about her political leanings and various ideas that excited her from a book they were required to read for a class they were both taking. She was shocked when, at the end of the meal, he made a comment that revealed that he was both very politically conservative and that he had not read the required book and did not understand many of the ideas she had been talking about over dinner. She had assumed that he was all the things she wanted her ideal partner to be, and when she found he wasn't, her interest in him diminished rapidly.

John Money, a well known sexuality researcher from Johns Hopkins University, has studied these "love maps" and suggests that they form very early in life. Some evolutionary psychologists argue that these love maps develop partially because our ancestors needed to "size up" potential mates and mate fairly quickly in order to increase the chances of producing offspring before physical threats (such as being chased by a tiger or other predators) occurred.

While it is true that different people find different qualities attractive, there are certain qualities that tend to appear on most people's attraction templates. In other words, there are certain characteristics that most people find attractive. In our close relationships courses, we often ask students what they find

22

attractive in a mate. We find most students tend to agree on the basic qualities that make a person attractive. Further, the student's lists confirm what researchers have found by studying many different populations. The factors associated with who we find attractive and who we don't are listed and explained below.

WHY WE FIND SOME PEOPLE ATTRACTIVE AND NOT OTHERS
Proximity

This one is so obvious that students actually have a hard time guessing it. We tend to find people attractive who are physically or geographically close to us. In a 1985 article in the American Scientist, researcher David Buss from the University of Michigan humorously made this point by stating that "the one and only probably lives within driving distance." Curiously, while we romantically sometimes feel that there is only one person out there in the world who is our soul mate, partners tend to live close together. This is not surprising since in order to find Mr./Ms. Right they need to enter your world somehow.

Physical Attractiveness

We tend to be attracted to people we experience as being physically attractive. No surprise here. Students have no problems at all figuring this one out. We also tend to attribute all sorts of positive appealing qualities to those we find physically attractive. Researcher Karen Dion calls this the "what is beautiful is good" theory. Thus, physically attractive people are often assumed to be more intelligent, more socially skilled, wealthier, etc. than those who are less attractive. This bias toward attractiveness appears to be broad, and not limited to adults looking for a mate. Research with very young children as early as a few weeks after birth has found that they will look longer and be more focused on attractive compared to unattractive faces. We seem to be biologically wired to prefer attractive looking people than unattractive looking people. While this seems to be true for both men and women, it seems to be especially true for men. Whenever we ask our students to list the qualities that attract them to a person, the men in the class

23

inevitably list physical attractiveness as one of the most important qualities, whereas the women list it as important, but less important than qualities such as a sense of humor, kindness, or intelligence. This confirms what David Buss found when he studied physical attractiveness in 34 different cultures around the world. Without exception, men valued physical attractiveness more than women across the cultures he studied.

Buss and other evolutionary psychologists theorize that our emphasis on attractiveness probably developed to ensure that we mate with others who are likely to be healthy and young, in other words, those most able to bear children. This might explain the gender difference in the importance of physical attractiveness, since men remain fertile much longer than women. Therefore it is more important for men wanting to reproduce to find younger (also seen as more attractive) mates than it is for women. For women, older man may be more desirable, as they may have more status in the group and are therefore more able to protect their children once they are born. We think of this as the "Donald Trump/Marla Maples" phenomena.

Similarity

In our close relationships classes, we often ask our students which they think is true: "Birds of a feather flock together" or "Opposites attract". Many students think that the latter is true, that we are attracted to those who are different than us. What research has found, though, at least for initial attraction and choosing a mate, is that we tend to be attracted to people who are similar to us. In fact, these similarities can be striking. Research shows that we are typically attracted to others who are similar to us in age, religious beliefs, education, socioeconomic status, and personality. Additional research by David Buss and others indicate that we also tend to be similar to our partners in number of siblings, birth order, and even ear lobe size! While there may be numerous exceptions to these rules, if you examine large numbers of people on these and a variety of other characteristics, statistically significant associations can be found on all of these similarities. Thus, we tend to look for mirror images of ourselves.

Complementarity

There is, however, some truth to the saying "opposites attract." While similarity tends to bring us together during the early stages of a relationship, complementarity tends to keep us together over the long haul. When couples have qualities that are complementary, they tend to make a good team. One person's strength might be their partner's weakness and their own weakness may be their partner's strength. So the qualities we are missing, we vicariously possess through our partner. For example, suppose you are very shy and withdrawn. Yet, you do feel a need to be with others and to feel more comfortable in social situations. By pairing with a partner who is extroverted and social, you can enjoy the benefits of being extroverted without having to become extroverted yourself. With your partner, you may be more able to attend social gatherings and feel more comfortable and safe than if you were alone. As a result, you might develop important social relationships and friendships that you might otherwise not have been able to develop.

Reciprocity

We tend to like people who like us. How attractive we perceive a person to be is altered by whether or not that person likes or dislikes us. Further, if someone is very attracted to us, we may eventually become attracted to that person, even if we initially had no desire for him or her. One of us had a patient who was very shy and socially awkward. Someone told him that a co-worker who he had been working with for several years found him to be appealing and was interested in dating him. After receiving this information, he found her to be much more attractive than he had thought during the past several years and became interested, for the first time, in a dating relationship with her. In the movie, "Crossing Delancy," Amy Irving's character was sophisticated and interested in literary men. But when the local pickle grocer began to pursue her, she gradually became more and more interested in him. He sent her thoughtful gifts and let her know that he was definitely interested in a relationship with her. The movie ends with her grandmother advising the "pickle man" to "be like furniture." In other words, the one who is always there, always demonstrating his interest in her, will be the one who wins her in the end.

Arousal

When people are asked to describe the person they are attracted to, they often describe the physical sensations of arousal. "When I see him, my heart beats faster and I can't breathe." When we experience this state of physical arousal in the presence of a particular person, we tend to find that person very attractive. This research finding was surprising to some, who thought that people felt attracted *first* and then felt aroused. But it turns out to work the other way as well, because we tend to mislabel arousal as attraction. This helps us explain romances that develop out of very stressful and potentially traumatic experiences. For example, several years ago a plane crashed in Sioux City, Iowa. The crash was recorded on video tape and the plane rolled over several times as it was trying to land, bursting into flames along the way. About half of the passengers were killed in the accident. Two passengers who survived the crash and who met during the tragedy, "fell in love" and married shortly thereafter. A less sensational example includes romances that develop during the orientation week for freshmen beginning college. Or romances that develop during vacations or out of town business trips. While numerous factors may play a role in these romances, arousal plays a significant role. When we are aroused we tend to misattribute the arousal and feel more attracted to and in love with another. A classic example of this phenomenon is a study that asked subjects to meet an attractive research assistant over either a scary and wobbly bridge or over a very safe and low to the ground bridge. Subjects who met the attractive assistant over the scary bridge (high arousal condition) reported that they found the research assistant much more attractive than those subjects who met the same assistant over the safer (low arousal condition) bridge. In fact, the assistant received more follow-up telephone calls from those in the high arousal condition than those in the low arousal condition.

This may be why we often seek out arousing activities with first dates. Movies, trendy restaurants, aerial views of cities, etc. may all increase our general arousal which may make our dates seem more attractive (or make us seem more attractive to our dates).

Barriers

We tend to want what we cannot have. This is what is sometimes called the Romeo and Juliet effect. If either internal or external barriers are perceived, then we tend to find the object of our desire more attractive. For example, someone who is seen as choosy and selective may be experienced as more attractive than someone who is not choosy or selective. External barriers such as geographical distance or not being approved by important others (e.g., parents) make the person more appealing. Parents often report that when they tell their adolescent son or daughter that they do not approve of their new boyfriend or girlfriend, the adolescents then bond more closely. When parents do not try to keep the adolescents apart, the relationship tends to run its course more quickly.

Expectations

We like what we expect to like. If someone we know and trust tells us that we are going to like another person, we generally do so. If we expect that a date or meeting with someone will go poorly, it generally does so. This may be part of the reason why many people end up with partners who are like their opposite sex parent, men marrying their "moms" and women marrying "dear old dad." Our earliest expectations of what it means to be a man or woman, and what to expect from a partner come from observing our parents and their relationship. Sometimes children of parents with a conflictual relationship end up in a difficult relationship themselves, because that is what they are used to seeing, what they are familiar with. Conversely, some children of parents with very strong relationships may have a hard time finding a partner for themselves because their standards are so high.

1. Proximity "the one and only probably lives within driving distance"
2. Physical attractiveness "what is beautiful is good"
3. Similarity "birds of a feather flock together"
4. Complementary "opposites attract"
5. Reciprocity "we like people who like us"
6. Arousal" we like what stimulates us"
7. Barriers "we like what we can't have"
8. Expectations "we like what we expect to like"

As we examine the potential goodness of fit between ourselves and a potential partner, what are the characteristics we commonly seek in a mate or partner? While physical attractiveness is certainly important, many other qualities are critical to our selection of another. Research has indicated that for both men and women, kindness and understanding is the most important quality sought in a mate followed by intelligence. The following is a complete list of the top 13 qualities sought in a mate broken down by men and women according to research by David Buss.

CHARACTERISTICS COMMONLY SOUGHT IN A MATE

Males	Females
1. kindness & understanding	kindness & understanding
2. intelligence	intelligence
3. physical attractiveness*	exciting personality
4. exciting personality	good health
5. good health	adaptability
6. adaptability	physical attractiveness*
7. creativity	creativity
8. desire for children	good earning potential*
9. college grad	college grad
10. good genes	desire for children
11. good earning potential*	good genes

| 12. | good housekeeping | good housekeeping |
| 13. | religious orientation | religious orientation |

The characteristics that are starred, physical attractiveness and good earning potential, are those that represent a statistically significant gender difference. In other words, men definitely find physical attractiveness in a mate more important than women. Likewise, women find good earning potential as definitely more important than men. This is consistent with the "Donald Trump/Marla Maples" phenomenon described earlier. It may also reflect the continuing view that men will be the primary providers for the family.

ATTACHMENT

Another important factor that contributes to whether we are attracted to someone is our early experiences of attachment, which form our adult expectations for the type of relationship we will have. As infants, it is very important for us to form attachments to our caretakers. These emotional attachments help to ensure our survival, because it is only through the devotion of our caretakers that we are able to eat and remain healthy. We develop certain styles of attachment very early on, based on our interactions with our caretakers (usually our parents). Research on these styles has revealed that people generally have one of three attachment styles: secure, avoidant, and anxious-ambivilant. In order to study these styles, researchers often use the *strange situation technique*. In this technique, children are placed in a room with their mother and then exposed to a series of different situations. First, a stranger enters the room and then leaves. Next, the stranger re-enters, and the mother leaves, leaving the child alone with the stranger. Finally, the mother returns. The child's reactions to each situation are observed. Researchers have found that about 65% of children are securely attached; they explore new things when their mother is present, display distress when she leaves, and are easily comforted on her return. About 20% of children are avoidant, seeming not to care when their mother leaves or returns. Finally, about 20% are anxious/ambivalent; they tend to seek extra closeness with their mother, but get angry when she leaves and are not comforted upon her return.

These attachment styles have been found to endure over time, not changing significantly. This is why our early attachments are so important for our future adult relationships. Research by Judith Feeney and Patricia Noller at the University of Queensland and others has indicated that the successful development and maintenance of adult intimate relationships can be predicted by attachment styles when young. Individuals who were securely attached to their caregivers as infants have the ability to appropriately trust others as adults and can allow themselves to be vulnerable to appropriate others. Individuals who developed an avoidant style as infants (often those who were separated from their caregivers) are more likely to distance themselves from others as adults and have a much harder time trusting others. Finally those who developed an anxious-ambivalent style as infants (often those who perceive a lack of paternal supportiveness when young), may have difficulty trusting others in relationships and often express the desire for commitment and dependence.

Attachment Style	Experience as Infants	Effect on Adult Relationships
Secure (65%)	Caregivers responded Constantly to their needs	Able to trust others and form secure relationships with them
Avoidant (20%)	May have experienced Seperation from care-giver	Difficulty trusting others, tendancy to distance self from others
Anxious/ Ambivalent (20%)	Caregivers were incon-sistant in responding to needs	Clinging and dependant, diff-iculty in trusting their partners

CONCLUSION

The answer to the question, do you believe in love at first sight, is yes! We do appear to be hardwired to experience attraction very quickly when we encounter others who meet our criteria for what is attractive to us. On the other hand, we can also become attracted to someone over time, as we learn more about that person and more about the kind of relationship that will work for us. While physical attractiveness is undoubtedly an important factor in attraction, it is certainly not the only one. We seek out others who are like ourselves, who meet our expectations, who are attracted to us, and who are likely to form attachments that are familiar and comfortable to us. Attraction, like love, seems to have its roots in earlier experiences within our own lives as well as in our evolutionary history. How can this information help in finding and keeping a healthy relationship? If you find yourself being attracted to people that are not right for you, it may help to identify your own attraction template and the early sources that help to form it. Awareness of the kinds of people and relationships you are "automatically" attracted to can help you to realize earlier on whether the person you are attracted to is really the best person to pursue a relationship with.

Chapter 4
Love

Defining love is remarkably difficult to do. All efforts seem simplified and superficial. Or, they seem to fall flat. For example, Webster defines love as a "strong affection for another arising out of kinship or personal ties." Not too exciting. Psychologists, poets, songwriter, etc. have all attempted to define, characterize, and understand love. Love is certainly multifaceted, individualized, and is influenced by many factors. What is love? What are the different kinds of love? Will love last forever? How do I know if I'm truly in love? These questions have been asked by people for thousands of years. A particularly poignant example of the difficulty of defining love is the interview with Charles and Diana following their engagement. In response to a reporter's inquiring about whether love was involved in their decision to marry, Diana declared firmly "Of course!" She even seemed a bit shocked that the interviewer would ask such a question. Charles, however, immediately followed with "whatever love means . . ."

LOVE MYTHS
A number of myths about love have been perpetuated for centuries. While most of us realize that these myths have little or no basis in reality, we tend to believe (or at least want to believe) that they are true. What are the most common myths regarding love?

Common Love Myths
1. There is only one true love for me
2. Once you are in love, all your problems go away
3. Love conquers all
4. Love making works out perfectly every time
5. Once in love, you will never find another person attractive and certainly never fantasize about another

---

There is only one true love for me.

We call this the Sleepless in Seattle effect. As you may recall if you saw the popular movie, Tom Hanks plays a widowed man in Seattle while Meg Ryan plays a single women in New York who find each other following a rather fantastic series of events. The film, like many films, suggests that of the billions of people who occupy the planet, there is only one special someone who is destined to be your partner. Your job, and their job, is to find each other. If you do, relationship bliss will follow forever. If you do not, you will either be alone, or be lonely in a relationship with the "wrong" person (who you may end up leaving in your continued search for your "soulmate").

Once you are in love, all of your problems will go away.

We call this the "happily ever after" effect. The idea here is that once you are paired with the perfect partner, all of your problems (whether they be financial, medical, personality, work, etc.) will disappear. You and your spouse will get along perfectly well and nothing bad will ever happen to either one of you or the relationship. This can be a particularly dangerous myth, because inevitable differences between you two will arise, and you will experience difficulties in life. If you buy into this myth, you may begin to blame your partner for your difficulties. Further, you may begin to take you difficulties as evidence that you and your spouse do not really belong together.

Love conquers all

As long as you are in love, then all problems can be overcome. For example, if you are truly in love then you can overcome long separations, chronic or serious illness, tragic accidents, etc. We knew one couple who both worked as professors and who took jobs in different parts of the country. They took the jobs because the jobs were good and difficult to find. Further, they believed their love was strong enough to endure the miles and the years apart. Ultimately, this turned out to be false, as first one and then the other fell in love with someone who lived nearby. They failed to realize that love needs nurturing, attention, and time in order to endure.

Love making works out perfectly every time

True love results in passionate sexual ecstacy where both partners seem to know exactly what to do to please themselves and their partners and always reach an orgasmic climax at the same time. Anyone who has studied sex, and indeed anyone who has experienced it, knows that this is not the way the human sexual response works. Yet, we want to believe that it does work this way. A mother, who had recently begun to explain sex to her young adolescent children, recalled her son's distress when he learned this. He told her that he had heard that men and women don't always have orgasms at the same time - was this true!?! When she concurred, her son was very upset. In his mind, as in many of our minds, sex should be perfect, as an expression of our perfect love for one another.

Once in love, you will never find another person attractive and certainly never fantasize about another

Research about the sexual fantasies of married men and women find that this is simply not true. But again, belief in this myth can be very damaging to a relationship. Those who believe this and then experience an attraction to another will think there is something seriously wrong with them or with their marriage, when in fact the experience is perfectly normal and doesn't necessarily have anything to do with the state of their marriage.

These myths, while exciting and wonderful material for movies, are simply not true in reality. Curiously, even though most of us realize this, we tend to emotionally believe them anyway and often behave as if they were true. Even knowledgeable, sophisticated, and experienced people often behave as if these myths were true. As discussed above, this can be quite problematic, because they result in very high expectations for relationships and certain disappointment when they don't turn out to be true.

PREREQUISITES FOR LOVE

Now that we have tried to note (and dispel) some of the most common love myths, we can discuss how a person can know if he or she is ready to experience love. While this might appear to be a silly question, not everyone is ready to fall in love. For example, one of us has been seeing a 40-year-old single female patient who has been desperately looking for a partner. She has tried numerous methods to find "the one and only" and often reports that she has the feeling of finding a needle in a haystack. On the surface, she appears to be putting in lots of effort and aggressively trying to do everything she possibly can to find a mate. Yet, upon closer examination, she is really not ready to experience love. She has a great deal of difficulty trusting others due to a number of tragic experiences with her family as well as previous intimate relationships. Furthermore, her expectations are unrealistically high about the "prince charming" she is expecting to meet. She is ambivalent about meeting a potential mate because she is fearful, has difficulty trusting and is terrified of being vulnerable, lest she have yet another hurtful experience. She is not ready for love.

Are you ready for love? Research has revealed some important factors that are necessary for a person to be able to be in love:

Prerequisites for being in love
1. Ability to idealize the other
2. Ability to hope and believe you are worthy of love
3. Ability to trust
4. Ability to commit
5. Ability to combine tenderness with sexuality

Ability to idealize

In order to love, you need to be able to see another person in an idealized state. You must be able to visualize or perceive another as being worthy of love and be able to look beyond the small irritations of daily living. Along with this, you must be able to idealize the relationship, to see it as worthy of your time and energy. Marital researchers have found that people are happier in their marriages to the extent that they are able to "glorify the struggle." In other words, they realize that marriage is hard work and doesn't always make them happy, but they feel

36

that the hard work is worth it. That in the long run, they will be happier for making the relationship work.

Ability to hope and believe you are worthy of love

In order to love you need the hope that a relationship can successfully develop. An important part of this hope is the belief that 1) your feelings can be reciprocated and 2) you are worthy of love. Without these beliefs, without being able to see yourself as lovable, it is difficult to be optimistic about any relationship successfully developing. One patient was unable to have a loving intimate relationship because her self-esteem was very low. Despite the fact that she was an excellent student, accepted into a prestigious graduate school, and an accomplished athlete, she saw herself as a "fake" and was constantly waiting for her professors and coaches to find out that she really wasn't as good as they thought. Because she believed that she was not worthy of respect and love (despite all evidence to the contrary) she had no hope for an intimate relationship and instead remained single, certain that she "deserved" it.

Trust

In order to love you must be able to trust another. When you are intimate with another person, you make yourself vulnerable. Intimacy involves confiding in the other, in revealing parts of yourself, physically, emotionally, psychologically. In order to truly love another, you must be able to open yourself to being vulnerable and trust that your loved one will not take advantage of your vulnerability.

Commitment

In order to love you must be able to commit your feelings to a person who can reciprocate that commitment. Commitment is a key ingredient for a relationship to move beyond the initial attraction into a deeper kind of love. Without commitment, it is very difficult to develop the level of trust necessary for a truly intimate relationship. We have known countless couples who have been amazed at the change in their relationship once they have committed (either by becoming engaged or married). They describe feeling freer as individuals and more satisfied with their relationships. They are free of the worry that their partner will leave them if they reveal something "bad" about themselves. This sense of security makes them much more comfortable in and happier with their relationships. It also helps them to overlook the small daily irritations that used to cause conflicts.

Combine tenderness with sexuality

In order to love you must be able to combine tenderness and compassion with sexuality. A relationship that is purely physical, purely based on sexual satisfaction, is destined to be limited. Tenderness and compassion for the other, within and beyond the sexual relationship, is another critical ingredient to a truly loving relationship. One couple told a story about when the wife approached her husband very directly, letting him know that she was very sexually aroused. She though he would like her more raw approach and find it sexually stimulating. Instead, he became sad! He was able to explain later that her approach make him feel like he was just a body there for her satisfaction. He needed to know that she wanted *him*, not just someone to have sex with.

WHY DO WE LOVE?

Why is love such a critical part of our happiness as human beings? What needs does love fulfill for us? Psychologists and researchers of intimate relationships have identified the particular needs that human being have that are fulfilled by intimate relationships:

Basic human needs fulfilled by loving relationships:
1. Companionship
2. Need to love
3. Psychological visibility (mirroring)
4. Sexual fulfillment
5. Emotional support system
6. Self-awareness and discovery

7. Experience ourselves as fully male or female
8. Share excitement in being alive and enjoying another

First, intimate relationships provide us with *companionship.* Though this need can also be filled by friends, family, and even pets, having a lifelong partner provides us with stable companionship that we can rely on. We are less likely to feel lonely or lacking in friends when we are in a stable, long-term intimate relationship. Companionship is one of the reasons most often cited by people for why they got married. Second, we all have a *need to love.* It is part of human nature to want to care for and love someone or something outside of ourselves. Intimate relationships provide us with such a person (or persons when the relationship produces children). Third, we all require *psychological visibility.* That is, we need to be seen by another for who we are, what we feel, what is important to us. When someone reflects us back to ourselves, *mirrors* what we feel and say, then we feel understood and validated. You can observe this need easily in young children, who are constantly pointing out the obvious to their parents. "Mom, there is a dog," or "Mom, Dad got a haircut." It is almost as if what they see and what they experience does not exist unless it is also seen or experienced by the parent as well. Though we don't need validation for the existence of the objects we see as adults, we do require validation for our feelings and how we perceive and organize the world. Having a partner who knows and understands us helps us to get that validation.

Fourth, we have a need for *sexual fulfillment.* Human beings are sexual creatures, and we need to be able to express our sexuality and obtain fulfillment for our sexual desires. Intimate relationships provide us with a partner for this important aspect of our lives. Fifth, we need an *emotional support system.* We need to know when we encounter stressful situations that there is someone on our side, someone we can turn to who will understand us and support us. Sixth, we have a need for *self-awareness and discovery.* Part of the development process, throughout our lives, is to attain a greater awareness of who we are, where we come from, and what our capacities are to obtain what we want in the future. There is no better place to really learn about oneself than an ongoing, committed relationship. This is one of the reasons why we enjoy doing couples therapy so much. Time and again, it seems that couples make progress very quickly compared to individual clients. This is because when you are in a couple, there are always two ways of looking at an event or a problem. Having the extra point of view can help broaden the viewpoints of each individual and help provide a more balance picture in therapy. Even though it is not always easy to deal with two conflicting viewpoints, it inevitably stimulates thought and often personal growth.

Seventh, intimate relationships allow us to *experience ourselves as fully male or female*. Being in a relationship with the opposite sex allows us to encounter their separate sexuality in a close and intimate way. It also allows us to express ourselves as male or female in contrast to our partner. Having children with our partner further assists us in being able to experience ourselves as father or mother. Finally, being in an intimate relationship allows us to *share excitement in being alive and enjoying one another*. When something good happens to us, we have someone to share our excitement, both because they love us and because when something good happens to us, it is good for them, too! Enjoying one another, one another's accomplishments, and the good things in life together is an important and very satisfying aspect of intimate relationships.

THEORIES OF LOVE
Psychodynamic

Sigmund Freud, one of the most influential of the early psychologist and father of psychoanalysis, theorized that we experience love because we are striving for our "ego ideal," or an idealized vision of ourselves. Feeling incomplete ourselves, we search for someone who will make us more complete. When we find someone who makes us feel this way, who makes us feel like we are a better person, we fall in love. Love, according to Freud, is also a manifestation of our life instincts (eros). This instinct helps to keep us alive, care for our young, and continue

40

the species. However, Freud felt that we are in a perpetual state of conflict between our life and death (Thanatos) instincts. Our death instinct helps to explain the self-destructive, aggressive, and hostile aspects of ourselves. We are torn between life and death, procreation and destruction. Our numerous films that focus on sex and violence seem to support Freud's theory that we are preoccupied with these instincts.

Other psychologists who followed in Freud's footsteps (neo-Freudians) developed the psychodynamic view of love further. In particular, Reik believed that love is fundamentally a search for completion. He saw love as our search for salvation, completion, and self-actualization.

Cognitive

Cognitive psychologists believe that love is not purely instinctual or emotional, but that it involves our thinking as well. In particular, Walster describes love as the result of feeling aroused in the presence of another *and* the way we think about and interpret those feelings of arousal (the cognitive label). Walster sees love as putting a cognitive or intellectual label on our state of arousal while with another person. We feel sexually or otherwise aroused when we are with an attractive person or with a person we would like to have sex with. We try to interpret this arousal intellectually or cognitively and conclude that if we are aroused, then we must be in love.

Another cognitive psychologist, Neil Miller, has conceptualized love as a secondary reinforcer. A reinforcer is anything that follows a behavior and causes us to repeat the behavior in the future. For example, when someone trains a dog, they often give the dog food after the sought after behavior is performed (e.g., sitting). The food serves as a reinforcer, that is, the dog is now much more likely to sit when you issue the command to sit, because sitting has been followed by food in the past. Reinforcers such as food and praise are primary reinforcers, they are desired for themselves. Secondary reinforcers are those that are not wanted for themselves, but for what they can get us. A good example is money. While many people find money to be highly reinforcing, the money in and of itself does us little good. The paper bills and metal coins that are money are worthless unless you can trade them in for something desirable such as food, homes, cars, vacations, etc. Therefore, it is the food, homes, cars, vacations that we seek and money allows us to obtain these desirable items. So it is with love. We desire many things that come with love: sex, understanding, support, etc. When we are loved, these things are provided by the person we love.

Biological

Many biological psychologists view love in more evolutionary terms. They ask the questions "What has loved gained for us as a species?" and "How has love contributed to our ability to survive and reproduce?" One such psychologist, Greenfield, conceptualizes love as something that helps maintain social norms. He reasons that love is a necessity in order to maintain a society that will maximize our chances for survival as a species. The activities and roles of husband, wife, mother, and father are very difficult and require numerous sacrifices. Raising children is one of the most difficult tasks one can undertake. So why do we do it? Greenfield suspects that love is what makes doing these demanding and difficult tasks worthwhile.

David Buss emphasizes the importance of the link between love and sex. He conceptualizes love as acts with the goal of increasing reproductive success. Therefore, love behaviors such as sexual activity, making a home together, and taking care of each other's needs all are designed to maximize the chances that our genes will continue in subsequent generations.

Solomon and Corbit designed a theory that helps to explain many different types of motivated behavior from drug addiction to love, called opponent process theory. The theory suggests that our bodies are designed to maintain homeostasis in all areas. That is, we do not wish to be too hot or too cold, too hungry or too full, too stimulated or too bored. We primarily wish to maintain an equilibrium. However, we enjoy a kick or jolt now and then. We like to break out of homeostasis and feel accelerated, on top of the world, excited. Because we are designed to maximize homeostasis or equilibrium, whenever either a very positive or negative experience occurs, the opposite or opponent kicks in in order to bring us back to homeostasis. As a result, over time, larger and larger doses of a drug, or larger and larger winnings during gambling are needed to obtain the same "high" we experienced when we first became involved in these activities. Our bodies just naturally do not want to remain in a state of high excitement for too long. Applied to love, this explains why relationships tend to be the most passionate in the beginning. The early passion in a relationship fades due to the opponent kicking in to bring us back to homeostasis.

Thus, when a relationship ends suddenly (just like when a drug addict suddenly stops taking a drug) a devastating effect or fall out occurs because the good feeling leaves so suddenly that only the opponent is left. Over time, again to maintain homeostasis, we feel better.

Additional theories of love

Lee conceptualizes love as having a variety of styles. We love different people in different ways. The different styles of love that he has identified include eros (romantic love), pragma (practical love), ludus (playful love), storge (love without "fever or folly"), and agape (love for God, for a cause, for mankind).

Abraham Maslow made a distinction between Deficiency Love and Being Love. Deficiency Love is the feelings of love that solve some problem for ourselves, such as being lonely or our need to feel that we are worthwhile because someone loves us. Being love is somewhat "need free" in that we are not trying to fix something that is broken in us by being in love with another. Instead, we love for love's sake, not because we couldn't get by without love.

Berscheid and Walster make the distinction between romantic love and companionship. They call the first passionate love. This is the love which is very arousing and motivating. It is the love that brings people together in the beginning of a relationship. The second type is called   compassionate love. This type of love takes more time to develop and is a deeper form of love. Compassionate love is what keeps people together over the long haul.

Robert Sternberg, a professor at Yale University, has devised a comprehensive theory of love involving three components: intimacy, passion, and commitment. A visual model of this theory of love involves a triangle with each component occupying the corners of the triangle.

Thus, for Sternberg, love involves the various components of these three parts of love. Different types of love are reflected by which components of the triangle are emphasized. For example, liking, such as in a friendship, includes intimacy and often commitment, but little passion. Romantic love, on the other hand, involves passion and intimacy without commitment.

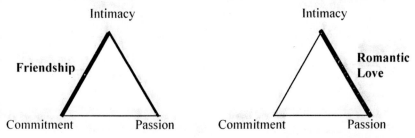

The third side of the triangle, passion and commitment without intimacy, is what Sternberg call fatuous love. People can also experience only one of the three kinds of love. Love at first sight or infatuated love involves passion without intimacy and commitment.

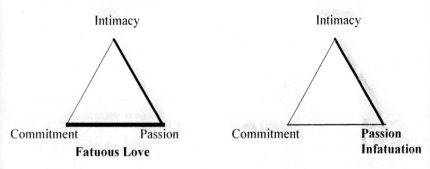

Empty love, for example, a couple who have stayed together for many years and who have drifted apart from each other, includes commitment without passion or intimacy. Finally consummate love involves all three.

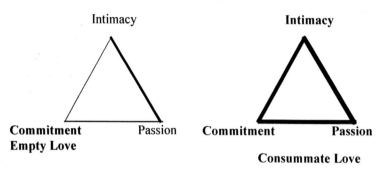

The importance of a relationship is characterized by the size of the triangle. The love triangle model can differ for an individual over time as well. For example, passion may prove more important early in the relationship while intimacy may prove more important later in a relationship. Sternberg has proposed an assessment method to evaluation your "triangle" in order for couple to examine the goodness of fit between each other, wherein similar triangles (or similar emphasis on passion, intimacy, and commitment) between couples are associated with relationship satisfaction and longevity.

CONCLUSION

Love is difficult to define and many theories have been offered to try to explain what love is. The work of many researchers presented in this chapter has focused on one aspect of ourselves in explaining love, such as our unconscious minds, our evolutionary history, or our conscious thoughts and emotions. However, in keeping with the biopsychosocial model, the experience of love is probably best conceptualized as an interaction of all these things. How and why we love in our lives is a result of our biological make up, our ancestral past, our own individual psyches as they have developed through our childhood, adolescence and young adulthood, as well as the social world in which we find ourselves (particularly the myths of love that exist in our culture). All these things work together to make our experience of love unique and deeply personal, yet with important similarities across all people.

Chapter 5
Sexuality and Passion

Sexuality is everywhere. Sex is how we sell cars, beer, perfume, movies, almost everything. We seem to be highly focused on sex. We are concerned about the amount of sex and aggression on television and in the movies, but this doesn't seem to change the fact that sex is what sells. How many people do you know who read the Starr report from cover to cover? Sex is what everyone seems to be drawn to. This is not surprising given Freud's theory about sex and aggressive drives (Eros and Thantos) discussed earlier. Are we biologically wired to be so fascinated by sex and aggression?

PREOCCUPATION PARADOX

While we are so focused on sexuality, we are also hung up by it. We are very concerned about who people may or may not be sleeping with. We are concerned about contraception ads on television yet our news is covered with the sexual exploits of our president. While we somehow feel okay about numerous sexual images and interactions on television, ads for contraception and other more "reality based" aspects of sexuality are typically prohibited.

We have observed this phenomena when we teach courses on intimate relationships. In a typical class period, there are often a few students missing, due to illness or scheduling problems. The classes are usually very active, with students asking lots of questions and making frequent comments about the material. However, when the day scheduled to discuss sexuality arrives, we see a definite difference in the class, whether at Stanford or Santa Clara University. Everyone attends this lecture, but hardly anyone says a word! Perhaps that characterizes the situation with sexuality in much of our culture. Everyone is interested but few will talk openly about it.

SEXUALITY MYTHS

Just as with love, there are many myths regarding sexuality in our culture. Even bright, sophisticated, and experienced people have myths about sexuality operating in their lives. While most people will quickly agree that they do not believe these sexuality myths to be true, they behave in ways which would suggest that they do believe them to be true. For example, a person may report disappointment following a first sexual experience with a new partner because it didn't go perfectly. They buy into the fabulous, passionate first experience often portrayed in the movies, when everything happens naturally and both partners have a completely fulfilling sexual experience with no reality-based communication whatsoever (e.g., "Touch me here"). Examples of sexuality myths include the following:

Sexuality Myths

1. Men just want to have sex
2. Fantasizing about someone else means you are not interested in your partner
3. Natural expert
4. Elderly people aren't interested in sex
5. Woman don't (or shouldn't) masturbate while men . . . well they just can't help it
6. You are responsible for your partner's pleasure
7. Sex is a genital affair
8. Men always want it while women put up with it
9. Size is everything
10. Sex is dirty

Men just want to have sex.

According to this myth, men are only interested in achieving orgasm. They are not sensual creatures and have no interest in the non-sexual intimate aspects of a relationship. In fact, they do not even really care who their partner is, as long as they can have sex! The truth, of course, is that most men value all aspects of sex, including sensuality and sex in committed, loving relationships. We also know that there are some women who sometimes "just want to have sex." We see plenty of evidence everyday that this sexual stereotype of men is not true, yet often people still proceed and make assumptions as if it were.

Fantasizing about someone else means
you are not interested in your partner.

According to this myth, if you find yourself daydreaming about someone else during sexual activity then you must be having problems in the relationship. Often people think they have done something wrong or hurtful, or fear they are becoming bored with their partner or uninterested in them sexually. In fact, daydreaming or fantasizing about someone else, during sex or outside of it, is quite normal and perfectly natural. Large scale surveys of the sexual habits of men and women have confirmed that most people engage in fantasy before or during sex, and that fantasies help to enhance their sex life. Most of the people surveyed are in committed relationships, and they have found that fantasizing, rather than hurting a relationship, can be a useful tool for keeping the sexual relationship interesting and alive.

Natural expert

When you love someone, you should know automatically how to please them. Sex should work out perfectly ever time. It is a totally natural act that doesn't need any learning or instruction. Couples who buy into these myths often experience sexual difficulties, because they are unable to communicate to their partners their likes and dislikes. No two people are exactly the same in their preferences and in what they find arousing. Certainly we know that men and women can be quite different in their desires. Further, never having been the opposite sex, it is impossible for your partner to know what is pleasing unless you tell him or her. Many of us know this, but somehow we still find it difficult to talk about this with our partners, especially in the beginning of a relationship. It is important to break through this reluctance and disavow this myth. Ongoing communication about sex is critical, not only so you can learn more about your partner, but also because moods and desires fluctuate constantly.

Elderly people aren't interested in sex.

According to this myth, once you reach a certain age you become an asexual being totally uninterested in intimate sexual activity. Though there may be a decline for some people in sexual functioning as they age, elderly people still have the same sexual desires and needs as the rest of us. We know of one older couple who still enjoyed sex regularly up until the husband died at age 92!

Woman don't (or shouldn't) masturbate while men...well they just can't help it.

Psychologists have long recognized the normalcy of masturbation in both men and women. Sophisticated surveys of the sexual activities of men and women reveal that masturbation is a common part of the sexual lives of both sexes, single or married. Masturbation can also be a useful tool for a fulfilling sex life, because it helps us to learn about our bodies and what we find pleasurable and can be used to teach our partner about our sexuality.

You are responsible for your partner's pleasure.

Particularly for men, this myth implies that if your partner didn't reach orgasm or didn't enjoy the sexual encounter, it is totally your fault. This can be particularly destructive because it engenders negative feelings about ourselves and our sexual relationship and can ultimately lead to serious difficulties. As the stereotypically liberated and neurotic character portrayed by Teri Garr in "Tootsie," puts it, "I know I'm responsible for my own orgasms!" Though humorous in the movie, it is an important point. Only we know what is feeling good to our bodies and it is up to us to communicate that to our partner.

Sex is a genital affair.

For those who buy into this myth, sex only occurs if intercourse takes place. Without genital to genital contact, there is no sex. Another version of this is that sexual intercourse is the only meaningful part of a sexual encounter. Everything before hand (e.g., caressing, kissing, talking) is just a prelude to the important part, intercourse. Without intercourse, the rest is a waste of time. We know, of course, that sex is much more than intercourse and that sexuality involves much more than just our genitals. This myth is destructive because it focuses us exclusively on intercourse and takes away from the important mental, emotional, and non-genital physical aspects of sex.

Men always want it while women put up with it.

According to this myth, men just can't get enough sex while women reluctantly go along with sexual activity because men demand it. On the contrary, most women enjoy sex a great deal. Further, among men there are differing levels of sexual interest and motivation, as there is among women. Desire for sex is dependent on many factors and changes from individual to individual and from day to day.

Size is everything.

The bigger the penis and breasts the better. Quality and rewarding sexual activity is associated with very large sexual organs. In actuality, surveys of large numbers of men and women indicate that size preference varies quite a bit from person to person. Further, sexual satisfaction is dependent on a number of factors, including emotional state, position, state of relationship, etc, of which size is a relatively insignificant factor.

Sex is dirty.

Again, we seem to have this myth perpetuated throughout our culture that sex is somehow dirty, ugly, sinful or wrong. Though many of us understand that sex is the most natural thing in the world, we may continue to experience inhibitions based on this cultural myth. To become a sexually healthy adult with a satisfactory sexual life, it is often helpful to identify the sexual myths that we have bought into. We can likely better understand our own personal myths and views regarding sexuality by reviewing our early experiences with sexual material. For example, how did your parents teach you (if at all) about sexuality? What were the family rules on nudity in the home? How was sexual behavior such as kissing and masturbation viewed in the family?

Freud scandalized the professional psychiatric community by suggesting that sexuality begins in infancy and not adolescence. He declared that sensual pleasure and childhood sexuality existed much earlier than people believed. Furthermore, he thought that numerous children experienced a premature sexual awakening through the experience of child sexual abuse. He later adapted his theory to suggest that childhood sexual wishes and experiences occurred more in fantasy than in reality. This is a critical change in our understanding of developing sexuality. It means that when we dismiss children's interest in sexuality, or, worse, punish it, we may be helping to perpetrate harmful myths about human sexuality that can limit our children's future sexual health.

SEXUAL DIFFICULTIES

Many people experience sexual difficulties at some point in their lives. Often a physical problem is the cause and it is important check with a physician for problems like impotence or chronic difficulty reaching orgasm. However, sexual difficulties can also be a reflection of problems in the relationship and conflicts about sexuality. Sex therapists have been able to identify many of the common causes of sexual conflicts:

Causes of Sexual Conflicts

1. Failure to engage in effective sexual behavior due to sexual ignorance, unconscious guilt or anxiety, or unconscious hostility toward the partner.
2. Perceptual and intellectual defenses against erotic feelings.
3. Failure to communicate.
4. Anxiety about intimacy.
5. Marital relationship discord.
6. Lack of trust.
7. Power struggles.
8. Traumatic experiences (e.g., rape, child sexual abuse).
9. Transference and symptom formation.

PASSION

Most of us want a certain degree (some more than others) of passion in their intimate relationships. Many feel disappointed that the passion that they experienced very early in a relationship seems to fade over time. Some even feel that the loss of passion signifies a loss of love. Of course, the reality is that passion does change over the course of a relationship. Typically in relationships, the levels of passion vary depending on our life circumstances. Some events lower passion temporarily (e.g., birth of a child) while others revive passion (e.g., a wedding anniversary). Typically the period of greatest passion in a relationship is in the beginning. Gradually, for many couples, passionate love transforms into compassionate love, a deeper, more stable, and more empathic kind of love. This doesn't mean we no longer experience passion. What it does mean is that what brings us together initially is not necessarily the thing that keeps us together over the long haul.

This change in levels of passion over time in relationships have caused some to ask the question of why we experience passion at all. One of the more obvious consequences of passion is that it tends to bring people together. Some evolutionary psychologists have argued that we are biological wired to be passionate because during the uncertain and dangerous lives of our ancient ancestors, mating needed to happen fairly quickly and efficiently. When we mate we are distracted and vulnerable. Further, it often takes many sexual encounters before pregnancy occurs. So in order to maximize the chance that the species would continue and thrive, we needed to be efficient about courting and mating. If too much time elapsed between meeting and mating, then opportunities for reproduction would be minimized. Therefore, some argue that passion is a biologically adaptive mechanism to propagate the species.

Another interesting theory regarding passion is the opponent process theory discussed in Chapter 4. You'll recall that this theory, initially developed to help explain motivated behavior such as drug addiction, states that our bodies are primarily interested in maintaining homeostasis. We like our highs, passion being one of them. But when we experience a high, in order to maintain homeostasis, the opponent of that feeling kicks in and brings us to a balanced state. In this theory, therefore, passion, as we know it early in a relationship, cannot last because our opponent feeling is being used to bring us back down to earth.

Therefore, we must maintain a realistic view of passion. While passion can be exhilarating and frequently experienced during the initial stages of a relationship, it, like the relationship itself, tends to change over time in various ways. This does not mean, of course, that we are doomed to live passionlessly in our long term relationships. It just means that the nature of our passion can be expected to change over time. It also means that periods of less passion do not necessarily mean that anything is wrong with the relationship. We do, however, have to continue to be creative and thoughtful about keeping passion alive over the long term.

Stendhal has studied the process of passionate love and has identified several stages we seem to go through when we experience it.

Seven Stages of Passionate Love

1. Admiration
2. Anticipation
3. Hope
4. Romantic attraction
5. Crystallization
6. Doubt
7. Second Crystallization

The following is an example illustrating how this process might work. Gina had broken off a five year relationship about nine months ago and hadn't dated since. She was just beginning to be interested in dating again, when her brother told her about an old friend who was also looking for a dating partner. She talked with her brother at length about his friend, John. John was the same age as her, very attractive, a loyal friend, quite intelligent and accomplished, and had a similar family and religious background. She was impressed by his description (admiration) and arranged with her brother to set up an initial meeting at a party. She found herself really looking forward to the evening. Her heart even started to beat faster when she fantasized about meeting someone new and dating again (anticipation). When the night of the party arrived, she prepared herself carefully and was pleased with the results. She had recently lost a little weight, had been working out, and felt good about her appearance and confident about the evening. He was late to the party, but when he arrived, she found that he was indeed very attractive. She casually approached him and they spent several hours talking. The conversation confirmed that they did indeed have a lot in common, and when he left, he asked for her phone number. She went home feeling great, because she thought this relationship might really be the one (hope).

He called two days later and asked her out to dinner for the next weekend. They went to a nice restaurant and then for a romantic walk on the beach. Gina definitely felt her heart beating stronger and was self-conscious when he reached for her hand, because her palms were sweaty. As they sat on some rocks, she was acutely aware of how close he was, and when he reached over to kiss her, she found herself very aroused and excited. He kissed her again on her porch when he said goodnight. She couldn't believe that he was so interesting *and* had such a nice body *and* was interested in her too! (*romantic attraction*). They continued to date for several months, and she found that they continued to really enjoy each other's company. As her birthday approached, she realized she really wanted to spend the day with him, but felt a little afraid. After all, they had not spoken at all about any kind of commitment. Was she the only one he was dating? Would she scare him off if she made it clear that he was the only one she wanted to be with on this special day?

She was delighted when he called and invited her out for her birthday. He made a picnic lunch and they spent the day together in a beautiful park. As the day came to a close, she realized that he felt the same way about her as she did about him. An intimate discussion followed, when they made it clear to each other that they were now partners, and interested in dating each other exclusively (*crystalization*).

As they continued dating, Gina began to feel concerned about the relationship from time to time. She had never dated someone so attractive before, and had worries that if she gained weight, or became less attractive, that he might not still be interested in her. In addition, they had a couple of fights. They were really no big deal, but it made her concerned that this might not be the right relationship for her after all. How could she know for sure? After all, she had thought her last boyfriend was the one, but after five years of dating it didn't work out. Should she get out of this one now, rather than find out it wouldn't work five years from now (*doubt*)?

They continued to date and to have occasional arguments. Gina found, though, that they were beginning to understand why they were having these arguments a little better. She found they could talk about it pretty well and even avoid some arguments before they occurred. She also found her fears that he would find her unattractive fading. He made it clear to her that he loved her insides more than her outsides, and as the relationship continued, she became more and more confident that this was true (*second crystallization*). Two and one half years after they met, John asked Gina to marry her, and she accepted joyfully.

CONCLUSION

Passion and sexual attraction are powerful feelings. They are often the reason why we come together (or not, if they are missing). They are an exhilarating, wonderful part of relationships and make us feel really alive. However, they are not always stable and not always simple. It is important not to buy into the myth that a good relationship is always passionate, always sexually fulfilling in every way. More important is to not buy into the myth that these are the only important or rewarding aspects of a relationship. In fact, most happy couples rank things such as friendship, humor, and empathy as more important in making their marriage succeed than their sexual relationship. In fact, it is often the case that if you put time and energy into other aspects of your relationship: keeping up your friendship, communicating honestly and regularly, and creating nonsexual intimacy, then passion and good sex will follow. Once the beginning infatuation is over, passion and sex are no longer the foundation of your relationship, but a delightful reflection of the deeper feelings and commitment that now make up the foundation.

Chapter 6
Commitment

Investment and commitment in a relationship means trust, dependence, vulnerability. It means more stability but less freedom. We typically make decisions in our 20's or perhaps 30's concerning who to commit to that is expected (for many) to be a decision that lasts a lifetime. Thus committing to someone at, for example, age 25 should be a good decision that lasts 50, 60, or more years.

At some level it is curious that people commit to a relationship at all. For example, many people marry fully expecting that their marriage will not end in divorce. Yet, 50% of all marriages end in divorce and not all of the remaining 50% of marriages are blissfully happy. Yet, we tend to confidently marry our selected partner expecting and certainly hoping that we will be happy togther for the rest of our lives. If we knew that we had a 50% chance of failing in education, or our careers, or having a good time on our vacation, I wonder if we would enter these activities with the kind of optimism with which we enter into marriage.

Some argue that marriage is an outdated concept. Some say that "fidelity is a tradition born of a shorter life span." It was only a handful of decades ago that people tended to have a very short life expectancy. Thus, marriage was expected to last about 15 years or so rather than 50 or 60 today. Furthermore, in many cultures, marriages were arranged or were not initiated out of feelings of love. Therefore, many people didn't expect that they would be in love with their spouse or that love was expected throughout the entire course of a long term relationship.

Often people do not realize that they do not commit to one human being but a whole family and system. In-laws, family members, culture, world views, etc. are all part of the package when we commit to one person in marriage or any other long term committed relationship model. Therefore, having some degree of hope that you can manage a reasonably satisfying relationship with your partner's parents, siblings, and other family members is important and shouldn't be underestimated.

Yet, despite the divorce rate, despite the myriad difficulties of spending a lifetime together, people commit and remain committed to relationships everyday. In fact, some people choose to stay in relationships even when they are not satisfied in those relationships, even, in extreme cases, when they are emotionally or physically abused. Psychologists have long recognized that commitment to a relationship and satisfaction with a relationship, while highly correlated, are not the same thing. There are couples who are highly committed to their relationship who are also very satisfied with it (probably their satisfaction is the main reason they are so committed!), couples who remain committed who are not satisfied with their relationships, and couples who are relatively satisfied but choose to end the relationship anyway. How can we make sense of this? Researchers have striven to understand the concept of commitment better, and to come up with a definition of commitment that can explain each of these very different situations.

Definition of Commitment

Researchers have long debated about the nature of commitment. Some have conceptualized it in a positive way, as an intention to remain in a relationship because it is good, satisfying and helpful for both partners. Others have defined it from a more negative perspective, as a constraint to remain in a relationship because a person doesn't think they can make it on their own, either financially or emotionally, or because they are afraid of criticism from others or of being alone. Jeffrey Adams and Warren Jones recently published an article on commitment, where they reported results from six different studies, including over 1400 married couples and over 350 dating couples, in an attempt to discover once and for all the most accurate definition of commitment. Their results indicate that commitment is three dimensional. That is, commitment is made up of three factors, some of which may be more prevalent at certain stages of a relationship than others.

Three aspects of commitment

1) An attraction component
2) A sense of moral obligation/Belief in the sanctity of marriage
3) A constraining force

The first, the attraction component, refers to commitment based on the value, attraction, and personal satisfaction derived from the relationship. This aspect of commitment is rooted in the rewards and pleasures the relationship provides that makes being in the relationship highly desirable and makes the individual much less likely to leave the relationship. People who are in relationships where this aspect is the most prevalent are highly satisfied, very much in love, more likely to make personal sacrifices for their partners, and like to identify themselves as part of the couple to others. They tend not to look at or value other alternatives (such as another partner or being alone). This aspect of commitment is both a result of being satisfied with the relationship and also serves to continue to enhance satisfaction as well. This is often the aspect of commitment that is most prevalent in the beginning of the relationship, during the infatuation stage.

The second component, a sense of moral obligation or belief in the sanctity of marriage, refers to commitment based on the sense that marriage is an important institution and the care and effort put into marriage is both worthwhile and morally imperative. This may also be linked to religious or spiritual compunctions that it is a duty to do whatever is necessary to stay married or to have a strong marital relationship. This aspect becomes more prevalent as the relationship gets older. As people grow beyond infatuation, they often begin to value the relationship more as a secure foundation which they (and their children, if they have any) can count on. They become more motivated to keep the relationship strong for the sake and importance of the relationship, rather than simply because of the rewards the relationship provides them as an individual.

The third component, a constraining force, refers to factors outside the relationship that may keep a person from leaving, even if they really want to leave. Factors that often serve as constraining forces including disapproval from others, financial difficulties, concern for children, or fear that another partner could not be found. This aspect is most prevalent in relationships that are in distress. Here, spouses are not happy with the relationship, but afraid to leave it for fear of the negative consequences of divorce or separation. One of us saw a client who was very high in this aspect of commitment. She had been married for 17 years and had been unhappy in the relationship almost from the beginning. In fact, she had left her husband in the second year of the marriage because he was emotionally abusive and extremely demanding of her (she had to have the house perfectly clean at all times and dinner on the table at 7:00 exactly every night, even though they both had full time jobs). She went to live with her sister for a few weeks, but returned to him shortly. When she came to treatment, she stated that her marriage was very difficult and she continued to be unhappy. But she never had considered divorce, nor separation since her brief one 15 years ago. When explaining why she did not consider divorce she pointed out that there were, of course, the two children and besides, she and her husband both really liked to play golf! It seems unlikely that she remained in the relationship simply for a golf partner, certainly there were other people she could play golf with. Instead, she turned out to be a woman with very low self-esteem, who felt she would be unable to get by on her own, and that no one else would ever love her. She remained in the relationship not because she wanted to, but because she was more afraid of leaving than of staying.

This definition of commitment was summed up nicely by M.P. Johnson, that couples stay married because they want to (Aspect 1), because they ought to (Aspect 2) or because they have to (Aspect 3). Adams and Jones coined these three aspects Commitment to Spouse, Commitment to Marriage, and Feelings of Entrapment. They suggest that the first, Commitment to

Spouse, is a reflection of current feelings of satisfaction with the relationship, while the second, Commitment to Marriage, is more like a personality trait. That is, it is a reflection of personal beliefs and attitudes about marriage, about keeping one's promises, and about the importance of living a moral life. Feelings of Entrapment emerge more when a person becomes dissatisfied with the relationship and also when more time and energy has been invested in the relationship. It becomes harder and harder to leave a relationship as your mutual investments, time, energy, money, children, increase. Just think how much harder separation is if you own a house compared to if you just rent an apartment. The more you invest in the relationship, the easier it is to feel entrapped if the relationship deteriorates.

Should I Stay or Should I Go?

Because it is easier to leave a relationship earlier, dating couples especially are constantly evaluating whether or not the relationship is right for them. Researchers have found that many people use a fairly straight-forward cost-benefit analysis to determine whether to remain in a relationship or to start looking elsewhere. They call this cost-benefit analysis the Social Exchange Theory.

Social Exchange Theory

According to Social Exchange Theory, the decision to continue in a relationship (or not to) depends partly on how satisfied we are in the relationship. To decide whether or not we are satisfied, we look at the benefits of the relationship (romance, someone to talk to, etc.) and the costs (loss of personal time, arguments, etc.). If the benefits outweigh the costs, we feel satisfied with the relationship. But it goes further than that. Each of us begins with an idea, an expectation of how relationships should be. One person might have had parents who had a very difficult and tumultuous relationship, and thus they believe that is how relationships are. They have rather low expectations for a relationship. Another person who had parents with a very fun and peaceful relationship might have much higher expectations for a relationship. According to Social

Exchange Theory, we take these expectations and compare them to our current relationship. If our current relationship exceeds our expectations, we are satisfied. But if it falls below our expectations, we are disappointed and dissatisfied with the relationship. Thus, what might be an acceptable cost-benefit ratio for one person might not be for another.

Consider the following relationship: Joe and Karen have been dating for about six months. Karen finds Joe very exciting and passionate and really looks forward to the time she spends with him. She has discovered, however, that he is not always very good about calling when he is late and often forgets to call her for days. She is pretty heart-broken when he acts like this, but still feels swept away when she sees him next. Her friend cannot understand why Karen stays in the relationship, she perceives that Karen is acting like a "doormat." For Karen, the cost of Joe's neglect is made up for by the benefit of the passion and excitement when she sees him. She stays in the relationship because her relationship expectations are consistent with her current relationship; to her, this is just the way relationships are. Karen's friend, however, has different expectations. She expects not to be neglected by her partners, therefore she wouldn't remain in a relationship like Karen and Joe's. This cost-benefit analysis can be written out into a mathematical formula:

Satisfaction = (Reward - Cost) - Comparison Level

But satisfaction is only part of the reason that people choose to maintain or terminate relationships. In addition, people also consider what their alternatives are and how much they have already invested in the relationship. If Karen met someone else who was just as exciting as Joe, but also more attentive to her, she would probably reconsider whether she wanted to stay with Joe. On the other hand, if Karen perceived that there were few eligible men around her and those that were there were very unattractive to her, she might more seriously consider remaining with Joe. And, as discussed previously, it is easier to decide to leave a relationship before much time, money, and energy have been invested than it is after you have both made serious investments in the relationship. A mathematical formula for commitment is then:

Commitment = Satisfaction - Alternatives + Investments

Therefore, we are committed to the degree that we are satisfied with our relationships (they are consistent with or exceed our expectations and the benefits outweigh the costs), that we perceive few attractive alternatives to the relationship, and that we have invested ourselves, our time and energy, into the relationship. This model of commitment has been found to work well in many different studies with many different samples. In one study, college students were found to be more committed to their relationships to the extent that they perceived relatively fewer members of the opposite sex on campus (verifying the importance of available alternatives to commitment). Another study demonstrated that this model of commitment seems the same for both men and women, and there is some evidence it may also be the same for other cultures, specifically, the same findings were revealed in a study done in Taiwan. An example of how Social Exchange Theory is used to determine how committed someone is follows:

Jane gets a number of rewards from her relationship with Mike. She finds him very attractive, they both enjoy jogging and bike riding together, they both enjoy participating in environmental protection causes. She likes being married and having the stability of married life. She enjoys her home and garden as well. The costs of her relationship include not getting along very well with Mike's parents who tend to be controlling and have never fully accepted Jane as part of the family because she is of a different religious group (being Catholic rather than Jewish like Mike and his family). She also has some trouble with Mike's habit of playing blackjack, feeling like his gambling interests are a waste of money. Furthermore, Jane feels that Mike is not that interested in her work as a nurse.

When she compares her situation with her expectations she is overall quite pleased. Her parents had a tumultuous relationship and divorced when she was 18. She is very committed to the concept that marriage is for life and feels that if she was not married to Mike she may not have an easy time finding another partner. Since she considers herself to be very shy, she feels fortunate to have met someone like Mike.

Will He/She Stay or Go?

Caryl Rusbult, a leading researcher who studies the social exchange model and how investment is related to commitment (the investment model) conducted a longitudinal study of dating couples to see what factors related to people deciding to leave the relationship (leavers) and people who decided to stay in the relationship (stayers). The following chart outlines the different ways the relationships changed during dating, comparing people who stayed in the relationship, people who ultimately left the relationship, and people who were ultimately left by their partner:

	Stayers	Leavers	Those who are left
Rewards	Increased	Slightly Increased	Slightly Increased
Costs	Slightly Increased	Increased	Greatly Increased
Satisfaction	Increased	Decreased	Slightly Increased
Quality of Alternatives	Decreased	Increased Greatly	Decreased Greatly
Level of Investment	Increased	Decreased	Increased
Level of Commitment	Increased	Decreased	Moderate

Rusbult found that stayers experienced increases in rewards, in satisfaction, in investment size, and slight increases in costs over time. They also experienced decreases in the quality of their alternatives. So people who stayed, though their relationships did have more costs as they went on, also experienced greater rewards and less favorable alternatives, and they became more and more invested in the relationship. Leavers, on the other hand, experienced little increase in rewards, a great increase in costs, a great increase in the quality of alternatives, and a decrease in satisfaction and level of investment. In fact, they showed a clear pattern of divesting from the relationship as they prepared to leave it. This may be one good indication of whether your dating partner (or you) are thinking of leaving the relationship; the extent to which your partner or you are beginning to reclaim things they have invested in the relationship (e.g., time, money spent on dates/gifts, emotional energy, etc.). Particularly interesting is the pattern of the relationships of those who were left by their partners. Those who were eventually abandoned reported fewer increases in rewards and satisfaction during the relationship and greater increases in costs. At the same time, their alternatives declined in quality and they invested increasingly in the relationship. "They therefore reported moderate levels of commitment and remained involved (albeit trapped) in their relationships until they were terminated by their partners" (Rusbult, 1983).

Factors That Increase Commitment (Kiesler)
Explicit behavior
People who are committed behave in ways that let others know they are committed. Telling others directly about the commitment, making large purchases together (e.g., car, home, furnishings), wearing signs of commitment (e.g., rings) both reflect your commitment and increase your chances of maintaining the commitment. People who do not engage in these behaviors are probably still considering whether or not they really want to make a commitment to the relationship.

Importance of behavior

Some behaviors are stronger indicators of commitment than others. Telling a friend you are committed to a relationship is one thing, bringing your partner home to meet the family is another. Likewise, a couple may buy a $250 table together, but this is certainly not the same thing as buying a $250,000 house together. The more important the behavior, the more the investment, the more likely a commitment will be maintained.

Number of actions

When instructing pregnant women about how they should behave during pregnancy (e.g., how to eat, what medicines not to take) doctors often emphasize that one single incident rarely causes a problem. Eating half a chocolate cake once during your second trimester, or taking one sip of champagne at a wedding is not going to cause birth defects in your baby. Rather, it is patterns of behavior that can affect whether or not the baby thrives. Mothers who drink alcohol regularly, or who eat only sugar every day are the ones who may experience problems. The same applies to commitment. One single action is less likely to signify a real commitment than a pattern of behavior. Acting in ways are consistent with commitment to the relationship over and over again increase the commitment.

Degree of volition

Of course, if you do the things that indicate commitment reluctantly, or because you think your partner wants you to, this will not necessarily increase your level of commitment. In fact, it may even decrease it, if you are doing things that are uncomfortable for you or that are making you feel trapped. Conversely, if you are engaging in the behaviors simply because you really want to, they will serve to increase your commitment even more.

Effort

We tend to be more committed to the things we have put a lot of effort into. If you go through some degree of effort or perhaps make some sacrifices for the sake of the relationship, this also increases the odds that the commitment will be maintained. Making a large loan to buy the house, giving up other important relationships to be commitment to one person, considering changing jobs or careers to accommodate the new committed relationship all increase the chances that the commitment will be maintained.

Degree of irrevocability

This is related to effort. When we make sacrifices or investments in the relationship, if what we do seems irrevocable, then we are more likely to remain in the relationship. An excellent analogy is deciding to become pregnant. Once this happens, and the child is born, there is no going back. You now have a child who will depend on you for the next eighteen years of your life. You are committed to that person. Likewise, if you take steps in your relationship that feel irrevocable, perhaps getting engaged or married, or buying a home together or even having a baby, this will also increase the chances of commitment.

Our attitudes also impact our degree of commitment to a relationship. For example, we maintain cognitive structures called schemas about many aspects of life and how the world operates or should operate. For example, one schema might be that "marriages should last forever" or another might be that "all divorces are painful, bitter, and should be avoided." These schemas or attitudes will therefore impact our tolerance for discomfort, for conflict, and will help to predict our degree of commitment to a relationship.

Conclusion

Commitment to a relationship is something that develops over time and depends on a number of factors. In deciding whether to commit, we consider how satisfying the relationship is, how bad the difficulties are, whether there are alternative partners available, and how much we have invested in the relationship. We also commit (and maintain commitment) for a variety of reasons. Some commit and stay committed because they are very happy with the relationship, others because they consider commitment an important, perhaps moral, thing, and finally others because they feel trapped.

Beginning and maintaining a commitment can perhaps best be done by "acting as if." In other words, if you want to maintain the feelings of commitment and the mental attitude that you are committed, then act in ways that are consistent with a committed relationship. Co-invest your money, your time, your energy. Show the world your commitment. Make your partner such a part of your day to day life that it becomes difficult to function without him or her. Engaging in behaviors like these will solidify your commitment and increase your chances for remaining committed for the long haul.

Chapter 7
Strategies for finding a partner

The overriding principle for finding a partner is to use the same strategies that you use to develop a career, find a job, or acquire an education, on your search for finding a partner. Many people assume or romanticize that the "one and only" will be found randomly in a single's bar, a gym, at the supermarket, etc. Most of us would not select a career, an education, or even a car by randomly looking for one without any plan of attack. While we often are planful and thoughtful about many areas of our lives, we tend to leave finding a partner to chance.

One of us had a patient several years ago who stated that her quest for a partner was "in God's hands" while she was working very diligently on making out a nursing career. She wasn't really able to make sense of why she felt that finding a partner was in God's hands while pursuing her career seemed to be in her own hands. Many people seem to think in this way which minimizes their chances of finding a partner.

Somehow we would like to believe that the one and only will somehow drop from the sky onto our living room couch and we'll then live happily ever after.

General Strategies for Finding a Partner
Let people know you are looking.

While it may seem very uncomfortable to broadcast to the world that you are alone and looking for a partner, letting trusted friends and colleagues know will often lead to possible matches. In the old days, it was much easier to know about potential partners before you made a commitment to a date. People moved around much less than they do today and stayed geographically closer to their family of origins. Therefore, people in the community could give you the "scoop" on so and so prior to making any attempt to initiate a potential relationship. Today, however, many are often anxious about who this person who they recently met and are attracted to really is. A serial killer? A psychopath? A selfish self-centered person?

Networking with friends and colleagues is a helpful way to let others who you know and whose judgement you trust to assist you in your search for a partner.

Be where people you want to meet are likely to be.

If you don't like drinking and the "bar scene" why try to meet someone in that kind of environment? If, for example, your religious faith is very important to you and you are looking for someone with a strong sense of morals, perhaps searching for someone in church related activities would be helpful. The key is to try to put yourself in environments where you are more likely to meet the type of person you are looking for. If you do not really enjoy the activities that you engage in to find a partner then each time you go and don't meet someone you will be frustrated and disappointed. Don't go to bars, the gym, church groups, sierra club hikes, the symphony or anywhere else unless you truly like these activities.

Consider dating searches and the personal ads.

Many people have a highly aversive reaction to the use of dating searches and personal ads. Many people feel that only truly desperate people or people with emotional problems use these services. While certainly many different types of individuals use these services, they can be useful and many happy relationships have started using these methods. Choose specific organizations and papers that are reputable. Investigate methods that will enhance your chances of being safe and in control. For example, consider not telling someone your address until you know them pretty well. Consider meeting someone in a neutral and safe place (e.g., coffee shop). Consider several telephone conversations prior to setting up a face-to-face meeting.

Know thyself.

Many people will state that they can't find someone who, for example, can make a commitment to an ongoing relationship. Yet curiously, they themselves are unwilling or unable to commit to anyone. Some state that they are always meeting people who drink too much like their parents and siblings do. Yet they tend to meet people in bars while they themselves might be drinking heavily. In order to meet and become successfully involved with someone, knowing yourself better is likely to be helpful. Use whatever methods you feel might be helpful to assist you in knowing yourself (e.g., talks with close friends, psychotherapy, reading self help books, prayer).

Develop an Action Plan and Time Line.

Write out your strategies for finding a partner. List the different methods you plan on using. While some may feel much more comfortable than others (e.g., telling close friends you are looking for a partner versus placing a personal ad in the local newspaper), list all possibilities that you can use and rank them in order of ease and comfort. Then set aside a certain number of hours per week that you will dedicate to searching for a partner. Write it in your appointment book. These hours could be spent attending an activity, buying new clothes, talking with friends about your search, investigating possible organizations and singles activities, etc. The key is to commit to a certain number of hours each week to this "job." Then, map out a time line for your activities starting with the safest and easiest to the most difficult. For example, if you attend a church singles group for three months without success in meeting a potential partner, then move to the next item on your list of activities such as placing a personal ad in the local newspaper. Give yourself a certain length of time with each activity before "raising the ante."

Specific Suggestions

1. Set aside three hours per week that you will commit exclusively to finding a partner. Do not let anything else encroach on this time.
2. Spend at least three months at each activity you attempt to use to find a partner. You need to give it enough time for people to get to know you and for you to discover whether anyone there might be a good match for you. However, if the activity or place doesn't seem to be panning out after

three months, consider trying another that might be more fruitful.

3. Tell friends whose judgement you trust that you are looking for a partner. Let them know the things that are important to you for a partner and be willing to meet the people they suggest.

4. Consider telling co-workers whom you trust about your search. Often people in the same profession are similar and might be helpful in identifying potential partners. Think of it like a job search. You would have a much better chance of getting a job offer if you apply for ten jobs, than if you just apply for one.

5. Join a church group. Singles often turn to church groups as a way of meeting people. Most churches have singles groups or groups for divorcees in addition to more traditional groups to assist the parish. You also increase the chances of finding someone who shares you values and beliefs in this type of setting.

6. Join Sierra Club hikes. This is another alternate place to meet other singles aside from bars. It provides an informal meeting place, focused on an activity (hiking). People in the Sierra Club are also often environmentally concerned and live active lives. If these things are important to you, this might be a great place to meet someone similar to yourself.

7. Go to singles Club Med. Club Med provides inclusive vacations all over the world for one price that you pay up front. Club Med specializes in providing a friendly atmosphere that encourages guests to get to know each other. Most people come and go at the same time (typically Saturday to Saturday), so the guests become familiar with each other over the course of the week. They also sit together at meals and share in many enjoyable activities (such as sailing, water-skiing, snorkeling, etc.). Club Med has vacation spots designed specifically for singles and promotes an atmosphere that will make getting to know people comfortable. Go alone or with another single friend.

8. Join a dating service. As mentioned previously, dating services can be very effective in matching you with other

singles and are being used more and more by everyday people who need a little help connecting with other singles.

9. Place personal ad in paper. Read personal ads in several papers and choose a paper that has ads that are appealing to you. Remember the way you represent yourself in the ad will affect the type of person who will respond. If you emphasize your attractiveness and sexual appeal, people interested in sex are going to respond. Be sure to emphasize the qualities that are most important to you as a person.

Chapter 8
Marriage

So you've finally found the person you want to marry and he or she feels the same way about you. You've set the date, told your family and friends and begin preparations for the wedding ceremony. You relax. The hard part is over, right? I mean, aside from a little stress and tension around planning the wedding ("Your mother wants chocolate frosting on the wedding cake?") once you and your new spouse exchange vows, the two of you will be off to a life of wedded bliss. That is certainly what many myths and fairy tales about marriage would have us believe. Most fairy tale characters endure incredible hardships in finding and securing their mate (she is locked up in the kitchen or put to sleep, he has been turned into a frog or a beast, etc). But once those hardships are overcome and the happy couple is wed, they then simply "live happily ever after."

Today, many of us realize that marriage is not so easy. Perhaps our own parents fought a lot, or ended up separated or divorced. Or perhaps we ourselves have experienced difficult relationships in the past or have close friends who have. It is becoming more and more clear that a wedding ceremony is no longer a guarantee of "happily ever after" (perhaps it never was).

THE PROBLEM OF DIVORCE

The study of marriage and what makes a marriage successful (or unsuccessful) intensified greatly around the 1960's and 1970's, when scientists became alarmed at the dramatic increase in numbers of divorces in our country. Though the divorce rate began to level off in the 1980's, the United States is still estimated to have the highest divorce rate of any industrialized country in the world. Today, estimates of the percentage of marriages that will end in divorce range from 50% to as high as 65% for first marriages, even higher for second or third marriages. In addition, it has become clear that divorce is one of the most difficult and devastating stressors that a couple (and their children) can experience. People who are divorced are more likely to experience mental and emotional problems (e.g., alcohol abuse), are more likely to be in automobile accidents, to commit suicide or homicide, and die sooner than people who remain married. Children of divorce experience lower levels of well-being, more behavioral problems (especially boys) and are less well adjusted than children whose parents stay married. Divorce can be financially devastating as well. In fact, single-parent households are estimated to be one of the strongest reasons why the number of families living below the poverty level remains so high in this country. Although few people would argue that divorce or separation is always wrong, it is clear that in general, couples and children are far better off if they can avoid extreme marital conflict and divorce.

In response to the increase in the divorce rate and the negative consequences of divorce, marital researchers set out to understand what causes divorce. They took two basic approaches. First, they tried to determine what made unhappy couples different from happy couples. Second, they began doing longitudinal research, following marriages over time, to try to isolate the causes of divorce.

THE DIFFERENCE BETWEEN HAPPY AND UNHAPPY COUPLES

There have now been hundreds of studies looking at the differences between happy and unhappy couples. Marital researchers have used many different kinds of techniques to assess the differences between how happy and unhappy couples behave, feel and think. Common techniques include asking couples to report their behaviors and feelings, such as in the daily diary technique, and directly observing couples' behavior, either at home or in the laboratory. In the daily dairy technique, couples record, in the evening, what happened that day (e.g., how often they kissed, fought, etc.) and how they are feeling about the relationship that evening. This gives researchers information about how happy and unhappy couples behave differently and how their behavior affects how satisfied they are feeling about the relationship. One major problem with this technique is that couples don't always report accurately, and their reports may disagree about such basic things as whether or not they've made love the night before! So researchers also observe their behavior directly. This is usually done by videotaping or audio taping couples in the laboratory or in the home. At home, couples tape themselves or having tapes set up to randomly record throughout the day. In the laboratory, couples are typically asked to discuss some problem they are having in the relationship for 10 - 15 minutes. These tapes are later reviewed by researchers and coded. Researchers evaluate both the verbal and nonverbal behaviors the couples display and code them based on content and based on emotion.

As a result of these studies, we now know that unhappy couples differ from happy couples in their behavior, their emotions, and their thoughts. Based on couples' self-report (using questionnaires and daily diaries) we learned that unhappy couples seemed to have higher rates of negative behavior and lower rates of positive behavior. Further, we found that negative behaviors have a much stronger effect on how spouses are feeling about their relationships than positive behaviors. These findings have been confirmed by direct observations of spouses in the lab and at home. The major results of direct observations of happy and unhappy couples are summarized below. Most of these findings are derived from observations of couples discussing a disagreement or problem in their relationship.

Unhappy couples agree with each other less

Compared to happy couples, couples in distress disagree with each other a lot more. They seem to easily take an adversarial stance with one another, immediately taking the opposite side of whatever their partner is saying. In contrast, happy couples more readily agree with what their partner is saying and are less likely to automatically offer a different point of view to their spouses' opinions.

Unhappy couples criticize each other more

Unhappy couples engage in a lot more criticism of each other compared to happy couples when they are discussing disagreements. They are quicker to point out any flaws their partner has and how these flaws are responsible for the problems they are experiencing. Happy couples are more likely to tackle problems as a team and try to problem-solve without being overly critical of either person.

Unhappy couples reciprocate negativity with negativity

When unhappy couples are experiencing conflict and one becomes negative, their partner is much more likely to respond to the negativity with more negativity compared to happy couples. For example, if an unhappy couple is talking about money and the wife accuses the husband of spending too much in a negative tone, he is likely to respond with a counter accusation ("Well, what about those $100 shoes you bought last weekend?"), or by being defensive ("I do not spend a lot of money. When was the last time you saw me spend money?"), or by withdrawing from the conversation. However if the couple is not unhappy, he might respond with an inquiry ("Really? I wasn't aware I was spending so much") or by letting her know that her accusation was hurtful in a gentle way ("Wow, that makes me feel bad. Do you really think it is my spending that is causing our financial problems?), or by problem-solving ("I know I spend too much sometimes, I guess we both do. Maybe we should consider an individual monthly allowance to keep our spending in check"). By not reacting to negativity with negativity, happy couples avoid the negative spirals and intense conflicts that are a hallmark of unhappy relationships. Unhappy couples, on the other hand, are much less likely to make attempts to stop negative spirals once they have started.

Unhappy husbands withdraw from conflict more

One of the most common negative patterns of unhappy couples is the demand-withdrawal pattern. In this pattern, wives act in demanding and critical ways, while husbands withdrawal from conflictual discussions, either by not talking or by physical leaving the situation. Of course, the more the husband withdraws, the more the wife chases after him, demanding that he discuss the situation. And, in turn, the more the wife pursues, the more the husband withdraws. Though there are couples who have other patterns (both are critical and demanding or both withdraw) and even a few couples who have the opposite pattern (he demands, she withdraws) the large majority of couples seem to fall into this pattern when they are distressed and discussing conflict. Though no one is sure why this happens, many men state that they withdraw in order to avoid saying something they don't mean or getting too angry. Some research suggests that husbands have a harder time handling the physical arousal they experience when they argue with their wives. So withdrawal is a way for them to calm down and handle the situation more rationally. Wives, on the other hand, feel a strong need to understand and process relationship issues and conflicts. They feel frustrated when nothing gets resolved and the relationship doesn't seem to be getting any better. Some researchers have suggested that women may more often be the demanders because they are the ones who want the change in the relationship. This may be related to the fact that, at least until recently, men have constantly reported being happier in their marriages than women. Further, working women today continue to take responsibility for the lion's share of housework and childcare. This probably contributes to women's tendency to demand or "nag" for changes in the family system.

Unhappy couples display more negative emotion
When discussing areas of disagreement, unhappy couples display more negative emotion, particularly contempt, disgust, and sadness. Contempt and disgust are expressed both verbally ("Well that was a stupid thing to do!") and nonverbally by rolling the eyes and pursing the lips. In fact, it seems that nonverbals (e.g., facial expressions) differentiate happy from unhappy couples even better than the things couples actually say. Sadness, particularly wives' sadness, is a strong indicator that a couple is unhappy. Though happy couples certainly experience and express negative emotions, they tend to do it much less frequently and in less destructive ways (i.e., they avoid expressions of contempt for their spouse)

Unhappy couples display less positive emotion

When discussing a conflict happy couples tend to use a lot more humor and laughter than unhappy couples. Humor can be a very effective tool for defusing a tense situation or for gaining perspective on a problem, and unhappy couples seem unable or unwilling to use this tool compared to happy couples.

Conclusion

One very important overall conclusion that can be drawn from this research is that negativity seems to be much more important in determining whether a couple is happy or unhappy than positivity is. So, while it is good to be good, it is much worse to be bad. One husband I knew decided to take his wife on a surprise romantic weekend for her birthday. He arranged a plane flight to another city, a fancy rental car, and a stay in a nice hotel. He also bought her a beautiful piece of jewelry for her birthday. However, when they were in the car, approaching the hotel, he got frustrated with her inability to read the map correctly and barked at her. Her eyes welled up with tears and the weekend got off on a very rocky start. All his positive behavior was canceled out by the one negative thing he did. Some researchers have suggested at least a 5 to 1 ratio of positive to negative behavior, in other words, it may take about five positive things to make up for one negative thing.

ATTRIBUTIONS - THE WAY WE THINK ABOUT RELATIONSHIPS

Researchers have also found that it is not only the way we behave in relationships that matters, but how we think about them matters too. The way we think about our relationships affects how satisfied we feel with them and how we behave toward our partner. Consider the following scenario. Jen's husband, Don, came home late from work, walked in the house, barely said "hi" to Jen and then went to the bedroom and slammed the door. Jen might think of a number of different ways to explain this behavior. She might think "Oh, he must have had a bad day at work," or "I wonder if he's mad at me," or "He's a real jerk!" You can imagine how each of these thoughts

82

might affect Jen's feelings about her relationship differently, as well as her response to Don's behavior. If she attributes his behavior to his having had a hard day at work, then she might leave him alone for a while to relax and then she might even make something special that she knows he'd like for dinner to cheer him up. If she attributes his behavior to his being an inconsiderate jerk, she is more likely to be angry with him and maybe even march into the bedroom to tell him exactly what she thinks of his behavior. Instead of a relaxing dinner, the couple could end up fighting all evening.

This is not to say that the answer is to always think positively or always excuse our partner's behavior. But research has shown that there is a difference in the overall way that unhappy and happy couples think about their relationships. Happy couples tend to explain their partner's behavior in a way that makes them feel better about the relationship, they make what are called relationship-enhancing attributions about their partner's behavior. In other words, when they are unsure about why their partner did something (especially something negative) they tend to give their partner the benefit of the doubt. On the other hand, unhappy couples tend to see their partner in the worst possible light. They make distress-maintaining attributions about their partner's behavior.

When a spouse in an unhappy marriage acts in a negative way, such as Don in the example above, the negative behavior is often seen as internal, stable and global by the partner. In other words, Jen will be more likely to attribute Don's behavior to his being a inconsiderate jerk. Being a jerk is something internal to Don, that remains stable over time, and that will probably affect other areas of the relationship. However, if Don manages to do something positive, like bring Jen flowers, she will be more likely to attribute the flowers as external (he must have had a really good day), unstable (he almost never does things like this) and specific (he so rarely does nice things for me at all). For happy couples, the opposite occurs. If Jen and Don are happy in their relationship, Jen would attributed the slamming of the door as a result of a really bad day at work, something external to himself, that happens rarely and doesn't really affect the rest of the relationship. When receiving flowers, Jen would think thoughts such as: "What a nice guy he is!" (internal), "He is often very considerate and thoughtful toward me" (stable and global).

THE CAUSES OF DIVORCE

Though we learn a lot about marriages from studying happy and unhappy couples, this does not really tell us how they got that way. Most couples start out very happy and satisfied with their relationships. But then at least half of them become distressed over time. The only way to find out how this happens is to follow couples over time. Researchers are beginning to take this approach more and more. They interview and observe newlywed couples and then wait several years to see whether they remain satisfied with their relationships and whether they stay married. They can then determine which are the factors present in the beginning that seem to lead to divorce and dissatisfaction later on. These studies have given us good information about risk factors, factors present at the beginning of a relationship that seem to indicate whether couples are more at risk for marital problems or divorce down the line.

The following is a list of risk factors, based on a review of all the longitudinal studies on marriage conducted by Karney and Bradbury. By comparing over 100 longitudinal studies on marriage, they were able to determine exactly what factors seem to be most important in determining whether a couple is high risk or low risk for future marital problems.

Risk Factor For Marital Distress and/or Divorce
1. Age
2. Income
3. Education
4. Parental Divorce
5. Relationship Satisfaction
6. Neuroticism
7. Stress
8. Physical aggression
9. Impulsivity

Age

The lower the age at marriage, the higher the likelihood of developing marital dissatisfaction or divorce. To put this information in perspective, the average age of husbands getting married today is about 26 and average age of wives about 24. It is important to remember, however, that this is a generality; there are certainly many couples who are older when they marry who end up divorced and many younger couples who do not develop significant distress or divorce. All things being equal, though, you've got a better shot if you are older rather than younger when you wed.

Income

Generally, spouses with lower incomes are at greater risk for dissatisfaction and divorce. In fact, receiving public assistance has been shown to predict worse outcomes in marriage. It seems likely that lower income affects marriage because couples with lower incomes encounter more stressors related to financial difficulties. One interesting finding with regard to income is that husbands' and wives' income and employment do not seem to affect marriage in the same way. While higher husbands' income seems always to be a positive factor, higher wives' income and employment seems to actually hurt marriages at times. There are several possible explanations for this, and noone is quite sure which is correct. One explanation may be that working wives actually experience declines in satisfaction in marriage. Another possibility is that wives who work have the financial means necessary to divorce their husbands, while wives without incomes may feel they need to remain in the marriage for financial reasons.

Education

In general, spouses with higher levels of education have more successful marriages than spouses with lower levels of education. This may be due, at least in part, to the fact that spouses with higher levels of education often have higher levels of income.

Parental Divorce

Spouses whose parents were divorced appear to have a slightly higher risk of being divorced themselves. One couple had a rather traditional marriage and often warned their children as they became teens not to date people who came from divorced homes, stating that children of divorce are less likely to remain married. Then, unexpectedly, they themselves divorced after 25 years of marriage. Their children exclaimed after hearing about the separation, "Oh no, now we have become the people our parents warned us about!"

Relationship Satisfaction

Perhaps not surprisingly, couples with lower levels of satisfaction with the relationship before marriage are at higher risk for future marital dissatisfaction and divorce. One person we knew had a tumultuous relationship with her fiancé, but reasoned that once they got married and were committed to each other, things would get better. However, what we usually find is that things do not get better, and these couples do not have a long way to go before their dissatisfaction leads to the decision to divorce.

Neuroticism

Researchers have long studied whether certain personality traits affect the likelihood of future divorce. Of all possible traits, one has emerged as the strongest and clearest predictor of divorce: neuroticism. People who are high in neuroticism tend to overreact to things, especially in negative ways. They tend to be very moody and experience quick shifts from good moods to bad at the slightest provocation. Now, most human beings do experience moodiness from time to time, or overreact occasionally. But the more a person seems to be this way, the more likely it is that the person's marriage may be at risk.

Stress

Couples who experience more external stress are probably more vulnerable to marital problems. An extreme example of this is the couple who loses a child. This kind of extreme stress often leaves couples unable to cope and can ultimately result in separation. Fortunately, many of us never experience extreme stress like this. However, to the extent that we do experience a lot of external stress (e.g., loss of a job, illness in a family member, frequent moves, etc) compared to the average couples, the more likely it is that we will experience marital problems. In their review, Karney and Bradbury propose a model that suggests that both the amount of stress we experience as well as how well we are able to cope with these stressors as a couple, will influence whether or not we stay together. One couple may experience a lot of stress, but be very good at coping with stress and therefore remain satisfied and stable. Another couple may only experience some stress, but are very poor at dealing with it, and thus end up separating.

Physical aggression

As we mentioned earlier, most marriages that end in divorce do so within the first few years. Recent studies have shown that one of the strongest predictors of early divorce is how the couple deals with conflict. If there are even slight incidences of physical aggression, or a lot of emotional abuse present in the relationship early on, this is definitely a sign that the relationship is at risk.

Impulsivity

One of the longest studies of marriage, which followed couples over five decades, found that in addition to neuroticism, husbands' levels of impulsivity predicted dissatisfaction and divorce. Impulse behavior includes things such as making appointments without thinking about whether they can be kept making decisions without considering all the consequences, and acting before thinking things through.

The Kelly and Conley study mentioned above is particularly important because it is the only study conducted over such a long period of time (50 years). Kelly and Conley measured a number of variables, including personality and family history, and then determined which couples were happily married, unhappily married, and divorced 50 years later. In addition to the finding that neuroticism and husbands' impulsivity lead to marital deterioration, they also found that the emotional closeness of the spouses, the amount of tension in their families of origin, and the number of stressful events they experienced all predicted how happy (or unhappy) couples were later. Using this data, as well as the data from all the other longitudinal studies, Karney and Bradbury came up with a model to explain why some couples stay together and why some couples eventually divorce.

MODEL OF MARITAL FUNCTIONING

In this model, there are three major factors that lead to marital dissatisfaction: problems or difficulties each of us has as a person (enduring vulnerabilities), stressful things that happen to us when we are married (environmental stressors), and our strengths and weaknesses as a couple (adaptive processes). More specifically, enduring vulnerabilities refer to anything about our individual character that makes us a difficult marriage partner (or, in the case of "enduring strengths," anything that makes us a particularly good marriage partner). These include things like personality variables (e.g., being neurotic or impulsive) and effects from our families growing up (e.g., a lot of tension in our families of origin). Environmental stressors are anything stressful that the couple encounters that could potentially affect their relationship. These include events such as loss of a job or illness in the family. Adaptive processes refers to how well the couple is able to adapt to any enduring vulnerabilities they might have and stressful life events they might encounter and includes things like communication skills and problem-solving abilities. All these factors are interrelated in affecting marital satisfaction.

One couple may have few enduring vulnerabilities but have poor coping skills, and that couple may become dissatisfied. Another couple might have a lot of stressful events, but have greater coping skills and remain very satisfied, despite all the stress they have experienced. As a result of all these factors, couples will either stay fairly satisfied or become dissatisfied. Those who become dissatisfied may then go on to divorce, though not necessarily, as there are many couples who remain unhappily married.

With regard to couples' adaptive processes, longitudinal research has identified several important aspects of how couples deal with conflict that predict whether or not they will stay happily married. Marital researcher John Gottman has identified four particular behaviors that predict marital problems later on and can be used as warning signs for future problems:

Warning Signs of Future Marital Problems

1. Complaining/criticize
2. Defensiveness
3. Disgust/contempt
4. Listener withdrawal

Of course, many couples will occasionally complain, act defensively, or withdraw from intense arguments. However, study after study has found that couples who do these things more, and couples who act in a contemptuous way toward each other and criticize each other a lot, are much more likely to go on to become distressed or divorced, than couples who keep these behaviors to a minimum. Longitudinal research has confirmed what we learned before, that is, that negative behaviors such as these can be very destructive over time to a relationship. No matter how nice you are sometimes, if you treat your partner badly, it will hurt your relationship.

Another thing we have learned from longitudinal research is that positive behavior may have a stronger role in preventing the development of marital distress than we previously believed. Studies that follow couples over time have provided some evidence that positive behavior in conflict discussions predicts later satisfaction. In addition, researchers are beginning to look at how couples support one another when one of them is experiencing a personal problem. This is a very different approach than the traditional approach of observing couples arguing. In the UCLA Newlywed Project, Tom Bradbury and his colleagues asked couples to discuss something about themselves that they would like to change. These discussions were videotaped and coded to determine which couples were better at providing support for their partners (and at asking for support from their partners). The results showed that couples skills at providing and asking for support from one another predicted future satisfaction even better than their skills at dealing with conflict.

CONCLUSION

Marriage has become an increasingly riskier undertaking over the last thirty years. Yet, people continue to marry at very high rates (over 90% of people marry in their lifetimes). Therefore it is becoming more and more important to understand what makes marriages succeed and fail, and to help couples to address these issues early on to increase their chances of success. Three broad areas have been identified as potentially problematic: what we bring as a person into our relationships (our backgrounds, our personalities), the stresses and difficulties we face as a couple (environmental stressors), and how we interact with our partners. We are often limited in how much we can control the first two, though we can make some efforts to address them (e.g., perhaps seeking therapy for difficult individual problems or choosing a career that is not too stressful). However, the ways in which we interact with each other can be changed. As a result of studies on how couples interact, marital researchers have identified specific techniques that you can use to help make your relationship work. These are presented in the next chapter.

Chapter 9
How to Make Your Relationship Work

LOOK OUT FOR DANGER SIGNS
Recall from the last chapter that researchers have identified specific danger signs that may indicate that problems are on their way. Specifically, John Gottman and his colleagues have identified:

Danger Signs
1. Complaining/criticizing
2. Defensiveness
3. Disgust/contempt
4. Listener withdrawal

Gottman and other marital researchers, such as Howard Markman, Scott Stanley and Susan Blumberg at the University of Denver, have been helping couples to identify these danger signs and to find better ways of relating to one other. In the book, "Fighting for Your Marriage" they present the communication skills and problem-solving skills that psychologists have used to help couples with their conflicts. What follows is a summary of this knowledge. The problematic behavior identified above usually occurs during arguments and help turn what could be constructive discussions about differences into major conflicts. If you see these behaviors creeping into your discussions, notice them! Try to understand where they are coming from, and used the techniques below to help keep your discussions safe and productive.

COMMUNICATION SKILLS
Teaching couples to have good communication skills has been a cornerstone of marital therapy for decades. You may recall about 15 years ago the well-publicized advice from marital therapists to use "I feel" statements. The idea here was to avoid accusing your partner when you are frustrated with something

they do. Instead, you were to focus on how what your partner does affects you. A good idea, but one that did not always work. Time and again, we heard couples using statements such as "I feel you are a jerk!" As you can see, just putting the words "I feel" in front of a sentence does not guarantee healthy communication.

Though that particular technique didn't always pan out, the concept is still a good one. It does really help to avoid accusations, instead sharing with your partner how you feel about whatever problem you are discussing. The idea is to see the problem as one that you share together. You are a team, and you are experiencing the inevitable differences that always arise between two people. As a team, you are going to examine them and work them out. Here are some tips for keeping your conversations focused, non-accusatory, and productive:

Tips for Discussing Conflicts

1. Avoid discussing conflicts when you are frustrated or angry
2. Make time to discuss issues on a regular basis
3. When speaking,
   a) Focus on yourself, not your partner
   b) Don't ramble, keep your thoughts short and succinct
   c) Allow your partner to paraphrase
4. When listening,
   a) Focus on what your partner is saying, not on how you would like to respond
   b) Let your partner know you have understood. Paraphrase.
   c) Do not interrupt your partner

When speaking, focus on yourself, not your partner

Tell your partner what is bothering you and why it bothers you. Avoid assuming anything about your partner's intent. Simply try to be as clear as you can about what is troubling you.

Psychologists have often recommended the following format to help structure what you say:

"When you do _____, in situation _____, I feel _____."

As an example, let's take the case of George and Jeanine. They had been dating for eight months and George had often been frustrated by Jeanine's phone conversations. Particularly, he got frustrated when he showed up for a date and Jeanine won't get off the phone - often for as long as 30 minutes. One day, George showed up after a particularly hard day at work, anxious to get to dinner as he had had no lunch that day. Jeanine was on the phone with her sister, waved casually, and continued to talk. George waited and waited, getting more and more frustrated and hungry. He felt as though Jeanine was being thoughtless and disrespectful of him. Finally, he left the house, walked down to the corner market, bought a sandwich and ate it. When he returned, Jeanine was off the phone. He told her he had already eaten. Jeanine got upset because she had been looking forward to going to the restaurant with George that evening. She began to cry and complain that George didn't seem to care about her very much anymore. George, by now completely frustrated, called off the date and went home.

This scenario is not uncommon and illustrates some of the basic mistakes that couples often make that lead to conflict. First, though George was aware of a problem for some time, he did not bring it up until he got really frustrated. Second, they both made assumptions about the other's behavior. George assumed Jeanine stayed on the phone because she was not very concerned about George or his time. After George ate, Jeanine assumed he did so because he did not care for her much any more. Both reacted to the situation, instead of waiting for a calmer moment to discuss the underlying issues.

Consider how differently things might have gone if George had told Jeanine that he was concerned about something, they had set aside a time to discuss it during which both were calm, and George had said,

"Jeanine, when you stay on the phone after I've arrived for our dates, it makes me feel like I'm not important to you."

Jeanine might have then assured George of his importance, and explained that her sister was considering filing for divorce from her husband and was often crying on the phone when George arrived. Having thoroughly discussed the problem, and understanding where each was coming from, Jeanine might then have made an extra effort to avoid being on the phone just before their dates and George might have been able to be more understanding when it did happen.

Keep you thoughts clear and succinct and let your partner paraphrase

When you share your concerns with your partner, it is important that you communicate clearly. One of the best ways to ensure this is to avoid rambling, and to stop and let your partner paraphrase what you've said. This way you can be sure your partner has heard you correctly and you can clarify anything that isn't accurate. It is important to avoid speaking for too long, because people can only absorb and remember so much at a given time.

Focus on what your partner is saying, not on how you would like to respond

Often our immediate instinct in conversations is to plan out our responses while others are talking. This is especially true in conversations with intimate partners when you feel you are being misunderstood, misrepresented, or even accused by your partner. Special effort must be made, therefore, to set aside your own thoughts and feelings and really listen to what your partner is saying. Remember, you'll get your turn shortly. In the meantime, though, you must listen carefully so that you will be able to paraphrase back what your partner is saying.

Paraphrase what your partner has said

Let your partner know you have heard him or her by repeating back what has been said. Try to be accurate, and try to highlight the most important thoughts and feelings. This helps your partner feel understood and relieves your partner from feeling he or she must repeat what has been said. Usually if you find yourself or your partner continually repeating the same thing over and over, it is an indication that the speaker has not felt heard. Paraphrasing accurately almost always ends repetition. Also remember to let your partner correct anything that wasn't accurate.

Don't interrupt your partner
Interrupting indicates that you are not really listening. Instead you are so anxious to make your point, you do not care to finish hearing out your partner. Being interrupted can be a very negative experience and put a bad spin on the conversation. Furthermore, it skips over the paraphrasing, an essential part of this technique. Therefore, keep listening until your partner is finished and be sure to paraphrase. Remember, listening doesn't mean you agree with your partner, but just that you care about your partner and what is important to them. Do be sure to take turns speaking, though, and avoid having one person dominate the conversation.

PROBLEM-SOLVING SKILLS
Clarifying and understanding one another's concerns and feelings can go a long way toward making the relationship work. It defuses potential conflicts and creates a feeling of being part of a team. It helps you to view the relationship as "us" rather than "you and I." However, some problems do arise that need more than just understanding. Especially as relationships grow and you invest more and more into them, differences will surface that require problem solving as well as emotional understanding. Examples might be differences in the desire for children or the number of children, ways in handling finances, or whose house to go to on Christmas. When these kinds of differences arise, it is still extremely important to communicate clearly as a first step. But once you know how each of you feels and why, a decision still has to be made. That is where problem-solving skills come in.

Marital researchers and therapists have come up with a series of steps that can help you to problem-solve effectively, and with minimal conflict:

Steps for Problem-Solving Discussions
1) Brainstorm
2) Identify which options are feasible
3) Decide on a solution and set a time table for implementation
4) Evaluate

Brainstorm

In this initial phase, the trick is to come up with all possible solutions to the problem, no matter how ridiculous. This is the time to be creative. Do not evaluate any of the options at this time, but just concentrate on coming up with as long of a list as you can. For example, if the problem is doing the laundry, suggestions might include taking turns each week, dividing the task in half, taking the laundry out to be done, getting a maid, or buying 30 pairs of underwear so you only have to do the laundry once a month. Anything is allowed at this stage. Take plenty of time to come up with as many solutions as possible.

Identify which options are feasible

Now that you've got a list of options, go through each and decide how feasible they are. You may not be able to afford a maid, or you may not have room in your drawers for 30 pairs of underwear. Evaluate the pros and cons of each option and eliminate those that really do seem impossible for you right now.

Decide on a solution and set a time-table

Having evaluated each option, decide on one that seems that most feasible. Then pick a time period during which to implement the solution. Two or three weeks is usually a good period of time for this. Set a time to meet after this period to evaluate your solution.

Evaluate

Discuss how well your solution has worked for you. If necessary, go back to your other options and discuss whether you want to try one of those instead. If you do, be sure to set a time table and have another evaluation meeting at the end.

STRATEGIES FOR ENHANCING
SUPPORT IN YOUR RELATIONSHIP

As we discussed in the last chapter, recent research on relationships has indicated that couples need more than good communication and problem-solving skills to make their relationships work. They also need to provide support for one another for the individual difficulties they encounter in life. Kieran Sullivan, Thomas Bradbury, Lauri Pasch, and Kathleen Eldridge have recently published some suggestions for therapists to help couples be more supportive of one another. Based on these, the following are strategies for couples to enhance support in their relationships:

Strategies for Enhancing Support in Relationships
1) Be aware of the importance of support
2) Learn to ask for help from your partner
3) Help your partner the way he or she would like to be helped
4) Avoid negativity, especially when being asked for help
5) Make positive attributions
6) Help yourself
7) Keep relationship problems separate
8) Avoid advice giving

Be aware!

Though we all have a sense that being supportive of our partners is good, we are not always aware of how important it is, and how good of a job we are doing. Time and energy spent being supportive of your partner will not only help you both as individuals to deal with the stress in your lives, but will also create a positive atmosphere that will make dealing with differences or conflicts a lot easier.

Learn to ask for help from you partner

Providing support for your partner and asking for support from your partner are two different things. Sometimes people who are good at one are not necessarily good at the other. In addition, research has shown that the skills required for each are different. Finally, effective ways of asking for support from a partner vary from partner to partner. The directness of the approach, the kinds of requests that seem reasonable, and the timing all may affect how well your request for support works. Make an effort to try different ways of asking for support from your partner and notice which approaches seem to work best for your relationship.

Help your partner the way he or she would like to be helped

We all have preferences for the way we would like to be helped and supported. Some of us like to receive emotional support when we have problems, whereas others prefer more practical kinds of help. In the movie "White Men Can't Jump," this difference, often found between men and women, was parodied in a humorous way. The couple (played by Woody Harrelson and Rosie Perez) were lying in bed and the woman mentioned that she was thirsty. The man immediately got up and returned with a glass of water for her. She started to cry. When he asked her what was wrong, she replied that she didn't want him to get her a glass of water, instead she wanted him to empathize with her thirst. She wanted him to say "I, too, know what it is like to be thirsty." Of course, Woody Harrelson's character was amazed by this. But the point was well made. The kind of help that seems useful to us may not be the kind of help desired by our partner. Perhaps for relationships, the Golden Rule should be re-written. "Do unto others what they would have you do unto them."

Avoid negativity, especially when being asked for help.

When someone requests help from another, it places that person in a vulnerable position. It is especially important not to be negative or critical at those times. Sometimes it is tempting with our partners, especially in cases when we've tried to help them and they've ignored us, to say "I told you so" or "If only you had done this . . .." It is times like these when it is very important to remember that asking for help can be difficult, and to be gracious and supportive. Otherwise, our partners may learn not to ask for help at all.

Make positive attributions

Our lives are very stressful today, and it is important to keep that in mind when our partners are distressed or come to us for help. Keep in mind that it is often the circumstances, not the person, that cause the difficulties. Making positive attributions about our partners' distress can help us to be more positive about helping them.

Help yourself

It is also important to realize that your partner is not always going to be available, physically or emotionally, to help you when you need it. Therefore it is important to develop other coping strategies for those times when your partner just can't be there for you. These might include things you can do for yourself (e.g., exercise, get a massage, take a long bath) and other people you can turn to when you need some extra support.

Keep relationship problems separate

Whether you are offering help to your partner or asking your partner for help, avoid bringing in any relationship problems you may be having. It is best to keep support and relationship difficulties separate. If you need support, but also have some related relationship problems to deal with, pick one and leave the other for another time.

Avoid advice-giving

It is often tempting, when asked for help, to respond immediately with advice. This is often not the most helpful approach, however, because giving advice implies that you are somehow smarter or more capable in solving your partner's problems than your partner is. Sometimes it is helpful to assist you partner in brainstorming solutions if he or she is stuck, but this usually works best after providing emotional support and validation of your partner's feelings.

CONCLUSION

Whenever two people live together and share important elements of their lives (e.g., children) differences arise inevitably. It is not those differences that causes trouble in our relationships, but how we handle them. How many times have you heard someone say, "We had a huge fight, but I can't even remember what started it"? It is these arguments that are destructive to our relationships, not the fact that we have differences of opinion. Psychologists have come up with techniques to try to guide discussions so they do not become damaging arguments. In addition, recent research has revealed that our ability to ask for and give support in our relationships is also a critical to maintaining successful relationships. Our world can be a stressful and difficult place. We need to be able to go to our partners to ask for and receive support for our individual stressors. If you are having trouble getting or giving the support you need, it is important to discuss this with you partner and find ways to increase the support in your relationship.

Chapter 10
Where to Find Help When You Need It

Many couples experience periods of difficulty in their relationships. Using the marriage model presented in Chapter 8, difficulties may arise as a result of environmental changes (e.g., having a child, losing a job, etc.), individual problems (e.g., depression, alcoholism), or problems interacting as a couple (e.g., lots of conflict and fighting, problems asking for or giving support). More and more couples are turning to professional therapists for assistance during these difficult times. Studies have been conducted to determine how helpful couples therapy is, and the news is pretty good. About three-fourths of couples improve significantly as a result of therapy. Long term, about half of distressed couples who come in for therapy experience lasting positive changes in their relationships.

Researchers are concerned, however, that some couples do not seem to be helped by couples therapy. They are working on improving therapy techniques to make them more effective, and are trying innovative approaches to try to help couples. One of these new approaches is premarital or relationship enhancing counseling. This approach is designed to prevent couples' problems before they occur. This helps prevent the damage that relationship conflict can cause and allows couples to work together on skills when they are happy, rather than when they are distressed and fighting. Howard Markman, Scott Stanley, and Susan Blumberg at the University of Denver are designing and testing a psychological intervention called the Premarital Relationship Enhancement Program (PREP) and have been testing it for over five years. It appears that engaged couples who participate in this program before marriage are much happier and experience much less conflict than couples who do not participate up to five years later.

Knowing that psychological assistance can help, whether at the beginning of a relationship or later on when you are experiencing trouble, the next question is, "Where do I go for help?" The next two sections offer suggestions for finding help, first for couples therapy and second for premarital or relationship-enhancement counseling.

COUPLES THERAPY

Perhaps the most important thing in choosing a therapist is to interview several potential therapists first to ensure the therapist is someone both you and your partner will feel comfortable working with. Often with couples, one partner is more hesitant about beginning couples therapy. It is very important in these cases to find a therapist who is acceptable to the more reluctant partner. For example, if a man is more reluctant than his partner, he may feel more comfortable with a male therapist. You and your partner should identify qualities that are important to you in a therapist and interview potential therapists to determine that they are right for you. The American Association of Marriage and Family Therapists (AAMFT; see below) offers a free pamphlet to people interested in beginning couples therapy, "A Consumer's Guide to Marriage and Family Therapy." The guide provides a great deal of information, including questions to ask a therapist before beginning couples therapy. The guide can be obtained by calling (202) 452-0109 or by visiting their website (address given below). What follows is a list of suggestions for identifying potential therapists in your community.

Tips for Finding a Couples Therapist

1. Recommendations by friends
2. Referrals by doctors/clergy
3. Practitioners identified by your health insurance plan
4. Psychology department of your local university
5. American Psychological Association
6. State Psychological Association
7. American Association for Marriage and Family Therapy

Recommendations by friends

As with any professional, recommendations of friends can be an excellent place to start. This is especially true if your friend has been in therapy with the therapist he or she is recommending. Your friend can give you an idea of how the therapist works and how helpful the therapist is. Keep in mind, however, that match is very important in therapy. Just because a therapist worked well with one person doesn't mean they will be a good match for you.

Referrals by doctors or clergy

Primary care physicians usually have lists of referrals for their patients who need psychological assistance. Physicians will also keep your request confidential, so they are good people to ask if you prefer to keep your therapy private. They send their patients only to other qualified professionals, and have usually sent patients previously, so they know if the therapist is helpful. Clergy are another good resource for referrals. They, too, will keep you request confidential and know many professionals in the area. If your religious beliefs are an important part of your life and relationship, clergy can often recommend therapists that work within your religious tradition.

Practitioners identified by your health insurance plan

Couples therapy is often covered by health insurance plans. If money is a concern for you, then beginning with therapists identified by your health insurance plan will help ensure that the cost of your therapy is covered. Of course, some plans will be willing to reimburse any health care professional, but others reimburse fully only for doctors and therapists on their plan. Further, some insurance plans, such as Kaiser Permanente, actually have a Psychiatry Department in which all their clients are seen. If this is the case with your plan, again, try to get referrals for a specific therapist. If you are assigned a therapist you are not comfortable with, you can request a change.

Psychology Department of your local university

Most psychology departments have lists of referrals for local therapists. In addition, many graduate departments that train future therapists run low fee clinics at the university. If you are willing to be seen by a graduate student or intern (who is carefully supervised by an experienced professional) you can often get very low rates (depending on your household income). Again, if you are uncomfortable with the therapist you are assigned to, you can request a community referral.

The American Psychological Association (APA)

The APA is the national association for psychologists. Most psychologists are members. The APA can connect you directly to the state or local referral service for your area. You can obtain this assistance by calling (800) 964-2000.

Your state psychological associations

All states have a state psychological association. They not only have lists of referrals, but they also know which therapists have received complaints by clients and which therapists have lost their licenses due to malpractice or ethical violations. You can use them for referrals, or for checking up on a particular therapist if you have concerns. You can get the number for your state from the APA or from your phone directory.

The American Association of Marriage and Family Therapists (AAMFT)

The AAMFT "is the professional organization representing more than 23,000 marriage and family therapists in the United States, Canada, and abroad. Since 1942, the AAMFT has increased understanding, research, and education in the field of marriage and family therapy, and ensured that public needs are met by trained Marriage and Family Therapists" (AAMFT Website). This organization can be helpful in finding couples therapists in a number of ways. As mentioned above, they provide a brochure, free of charge, that assists consumers in identifying potential therapists and the important questions to ask them before beginning therapy. Members of the AAMFT (the therapists they recommend) must meet training and education requirements before they are recognized as Marriage and Family Therapists (MFTs). You can get referrals and information at their website (www.aamft.org) or by calling (202) 452-0109. The website also contains a referral directory, where you can type in your city and state and receive a list of MFTs in your area.

PREMARITAL AND
RELATIONSHIP ENHANCEMENT COUNSELING

The majority of couples currently receive this type of counseling through their churches and synagogues. For some, premarital counseling is mandatory. For example, the Catholic Church requires participation in premarital programs before a couple can be married in the Church. Other churches and synagogues make premarital counseling available for couples who are interested or who seem to need it. These programs vary a lot from place to place in number of hours, the type of person(s) leading the programs, and the content of the program. As with most counseling, it is always good to talk to people who have already gone through a program to get an idea of how helpful it was.

A second resource for premarital counseling is therapists in your area. More and more couples are arranging for short-term counseling to help them prepare for marriage or to explore and strengthen their relationships. Typically, couples meet with a therapist for about 6-12 sessions, once a week. Look for therapists who specialize in working with couples (see suggestion in couples therapy section above)

A third resource is psychological programs designed specifically for preparing couples for marriage. Though these are relatively new and therefore not always easy to find, they are becoming more and more common. The most well-known program, PREP, is based in Denver, but therapists and ministers come from all over the country to be trained in this approach. You can find out if there are therapists or ministers in your community trained in the PREP approach by writing to:

Fighting for Your Marriage
c/o PREP, Inc.
P.O. Box 102530
Denver, Colorado 80250-2530

The authors have also summarized their approach in a book, "Fighting for Your Marriage" which explains the concepts important to building a strong, long-lasting relationship and provides exercises for couples to practice important relationship skills at home.

About the Authors

Thomas Plante is an Associate Professor and Chair of Psychology at Santa Clara University, a Clinical Associate Professor of Psychiatry and Behavioral Sciences at Stanford University, and a Consulting Associate Professor of Education at Stanford University. He is a licensed psychologist and Diplomate in Clinical Psychology from the American Board of Professional Psychology. He has published over 70 professional articles on topics such as intimate relationships, coping with stress, and personality. He has over 15 years of experience as a psychotherapist working with individuals and couples with relationship concerns. He has authored several professional books including "Contemporary Clinical Psychology," a clinical psychology textbook recently published by Wiley, and "Bless Me Father for I Have Sinned: Perspectives on Sexual Abuse Committed by Roman Catholic Priests" published by Greenwood. He has taught a course entitled, "Intimate Relationships" at Stanford University each year since 1988.

He obtained an Sc.B. degree in Psychology with honors from Brown University, M.A. and Ph.D. degrees in Clinical Psychology with honors from the University of Kansas, and completed a clinical internship and postdoctoral fellowship in Clinical and Health Psychology at Yale University.

Kieran Sullivan is an Assistant Professor of Psychology at Santa Clara University. She is a clinical psychologist who has focused on intimate relationships in her research and clinical work. She worked for six years on the UCLA Project on Newlywed Marriage, studying the factors that are present at the beginning of a relationship that predict divorce and dissatisfaction up to five years later. She has published professional articles on topics such as couples therapy, premarital counseling, and predictors of divorce. She has also taught a course entitled "Close Relationships" at Santa Clara University and Loyola Marymount University.

She obtained a B.A. degree in Psychology with honors at Loyola Marymount University, M.A. and Ph.D. degrees in Clinical Psychology from the University of California, Los Angeles and completed a clinical internship at Kaiser Permanente in Los Angeles, where she implemented a new program for couples to assist them in their relationships and prevent future dissatisfaction and divorce.

Printed in the United States
20876LVS00001B/1-42